My Faith, My Life

A Teen's Guide to the Episcopal Church

Jenifer Gamber

Morehouse Publishing, 4775 Linglestown Road, Harrisburg, PA 11112

Morehouse Publishing, 445 Fifth Avenue, New York, NY 10016

Morehouse Publishing is an imprint of Church Publishing Incorporated.

Cover art & design: Wesley Hoke

Printed in the United States of America

11 12 13 14 10 9 8 7

To Ed, with whom I walk in faith and
see the beauty of creation.

Sssh

Sssh the sea says
sssh the small waves at the shore say, sssh
not so violent, not
so remarkable.
Sssh
say the tips of the waves
crowding around the headland's surf.
Sssh
they say to people
this is *our* earth,
our eternity.

—Rolf Jacobsen

Contents

Acknowledgments

As I reflect about why I wrote a book about the Episcopal Church for teenagers, I have to begin with Christ Church, Poughkeepsie, New York, my original community of faith. It's where I was baptized and where I learned about God's love, Jesus' example and sacrifice, and the ministry that, as children of God, we all share. Our experiences as children and teenagers greatly form who we are as adults. The rectors at Christ Church, and more importantly the laypeople, embraced the ministry of each person—adult and child alike. The people at Christ Church gave me my first job—as counselor for an inner-city summer camp. Christ Church was my first public speaking engagement—as teenage homilist the morning after an all-night youth gathering. They taught me how to serve others—beginning with seeing Christ in one another to seeking Christ in our neighbors both close and far away. Christ Church sent me to the first Episcopal Youth Event in 1982 and supported me on a trip to serve at a children's home in Panama City, Panama. All of this while I was a teenager! I would especially like to acknowledge my parents, Loyd and Cynthia Lee, our community's rectors, John Kater and Michael Philips, and my dear Sunday school teachers, especially Julia Dutton, whose love for drama brought countless biblical stories alive. Their love for all people and belief in community created in me soil rich enough to bring blossom to the seeds of faith.

My current faith community at the Cathedral Church of the Nativity in Bethlehem, Pennsylvania continues to nourish me with great friendship, rich worship, and continued opportunities to serve others—especially young people. The idea for this book was hatched in early discussions with Anne Kitch. She also introduced me to Nancy Fitzgerald at Morehouse. Dear friends Beth Vorosmarti and Janet Kolepp kept my heart full with inspiration and my mind full with suggestions for revision. Abiding friend Meg Seltzer brought much needed levity with her wit and grounding with her sensibility. Jane Teter, María Tjeltveit, Barbara Gray, and Thom Chu provided helpful comments.

The Church Divinity School of the Pacific's Center for Anglican Learning and Leadership has been a wonderful resource. In particular, John Kater's course on ministry and Sylvia Swainey's course on gifts and discernment introduced me to a wealth of literature and ideas that have guided portions of this book. Both John and Sylvia graciously read chapters of the book and offered valuable suggestions for improvement.

Rick Cluett, retired Archdeacon for the Diocese of Bethlehem and interim Dean and Rector for the Cathedral, brought his gentle way, deep experience, and keen eye to guide my thinking at crucial places. I am greatly indebted to the wisdom and friendship of Paul Marshall, Bishop of the Diocese of Bethlehem, whose commitment to youth and to the spreading of God's love and mercy is evident in his writings and servant leadership. His close reading and subsequent recommendations strengthened the book.

I want to express my great appreciation for the friendship and very capable editorial skills of Nancy Fitzgerald, my editor at Morehouse. She understood my vision for a book that teenagers could read and understand—one that would share the beauty of the Episcopal Church and empower them to take their place. She lifted my spirits in the thick of sometimes difficult chapters. More importantly, she brought her knowledge and experience of writing for teenagers, challenging me at every turn to write both more clearly and simply. I am grateful for the creative hands of Dorothy Thompson Perez, whose illustrations clarify what is sometimes difficult to express with words alone. Ryan Masteller ably guided the text through production.

My greatest appreciation is for my family—my two teenage children, William and Emily, and my husband, Ed. William and Emily's laughter reminds me of God's delight. Ed's steadfast love grounds me. Ed has kept our family going while I've been squirreled away in front of my computer surrounded by stacks of books. I have learned much from him about how to live faith in the world. I thank God for every day we share together.

Foreword

by Katharine Jefferts Schori

As you begin to explore this guide, Jenifer Gamber will ask you to read it "with curiosity, an open heart, and a critical eye." May the tools this book offers help you commit yourself to a life that is defined by a hunger for that same burning curiosity, open heart, and critical eye. As you begin to explore your questions about faith and your role in the world, I hope you will discover some of the great riches of our faith. Those riches can lead to a full and growing faith that will do two things—bring you closer to God and invite a deeper love of all God's children, whatever their age, gender, color, nationality, or faith.

The curiosity and hunger you bring to this journey are an invitation. Amazing things are possible when we are willing to open ourselves to the light of Christ and, in turn, begin to become that light. Baptism joins us to the gospel work of receiving God's transforming grace and the creative work of becoming an instrument of transformation in the world. When we say the "yes" of baptism, we are affirming our own part in fulfilling God's vision of a healed world. We are transformed by faith in order to transform the world. Jesus talked about that transformed world as the Reign of God (Kingdom of God in some Bibles). That vision of the Reign of God is what Jesus claims as his own mission (see Luke 4:16–21). If God is in charge, then all people have enough to eat, disease and mental illness are healed, and people live together in peace and justice. If you look around, you'll see that we still have work to do—we're not there yet!

After reading this guide, how will you begin to work toward transforming this world? What can you do—with your friends, in your congregation or school, to help to see that all people have enough to eat or medical care when illness strikes? How can you help to bring peace to your corner of the schoolyard or across the globe?

The light of Christ that shines in you can help to banish the darkness of this world. This journey we're on as the Church is an exciting adventure, and I pray that this book can help you discover some more of that wonderful adventure. It is a journey that stretches out before us for all the years of our lives, we have great companions, and we only have to put our feet on the path.

May God's blessing go with you, may the light of Christ illumine your way, and may the wind of Holy Spirit speed your journey!

Katharine Jefferts Schori
Presiding Bishop and Primate
The Episcopal Church

Introduction

FOR TEENS

By title and design, this book invites you to ask the deepest questions—questions of God, questions of promise, questions of belief. Did you ever wonder, "Why read the Bible?" or "What is the church?" or as a young person, "How are my leadership and gifts accepted in the Episcopal Church?"

Jenifer Gamber has developed this guide for you to ask your own deepest questions, and sets them in the context of history, tradition, and reason that reaches from the early church to today. How you use this guide is limited only by your imagination—you'll discover ways to reflect on your own relationship with God, with your community, and even with your friends and classmates who take this journey with you.

In this book, Jenifer invites you—and I invite you, too—to consider this question: Where is my ministry? What does it look like? What are my gifts to share? In this guide and through your reflection you will discover a variety of answers to these and other questions by actively responding to Scripture passages, to the lives of saints, and even to music and video. It's amazing what the movie *The Incredibles* can say to you about your faith! In the least likely places you'll discover the many gifts that you can use to do good in the world in the name of the love of God. In this book you will discover this and much more.

So take this text and risk a new step on your journey. Bring your real self to this experience and, along with the other teens in your group or class, you just might discover a new awareness of your growing faith.

Remember, "The church community is with you to help you keep your promise of Baptism." We need you to share the journey with us, too. Together, after all, we are the body of the living Christ. We all are the church.

FOR PARENTS AND EDUCATORS

Youth and young adulthood are currently a passionate preoccupation of the Episcopal Church. The 2003 General Convention set the pace through creating and passing resolutions and budget that focused on the urgency of faith formation and development with our young people. Every congregation in the church's "Call to Grow" is concerned with nurturing youth in their faith, and every diocese seeks to provide opportunities to examine all the ways to reach our young people in a postmodern age.

This accent on youth is a reflection of the reality of the age crises that face the church. On the surface there is an absolute drive for survival as congregations age and begin to consider how will we keep alive the traditions and history of the church. Below the surface there is a deep awareness of the importance of our identity as Christians who worship in the Episcopal tradition. It is to the depth that Jenifer Gamber has crafted this wonderful and much needed resource, *My Faith, My Life: A Teen's Guide to the Episcopal Church.* Unique in its pedagogical approach and design, offers mentors, parents, youth leaders, and confirmation instructors an alternative that provides a missionary impetus for sharing the history, tradition, and reason with our teens.

The resource descends through the waters of baptism to surface on the development of faith from the early church to postmodern culture. Active voices provide inspiration to teens who are led by the promise, "God is with you to strengthen you to keep the promises" and "The church community is with you to help you keep your promise." I can only imagine what youth ministry might look like if this resource is taken seriously. For it expects and honors the dignity of our young people in their quest not only for knowledge but to know the living Christ in their heart.

It is a critical time in the life of our church to consider the place of identity, authority and vocation in the lives of our young people through this historical experiential resource designed to reach those in the life of the church who seek to discover what is this church I belong to? And who am I in it?

Robyn Szoke
Associate Rector, St. John's Episcopal Church
Carlisle, Pennsylvania

How to Read This Book

I hope you read this book like you would any other—with curiosity, an open heart, and a critical eye. I invite you to think about what you read, ask questions, and determine for yourself ultimately what you believe.

Throughout the book you'll find a guide to help you along your journey. Notes in the margin and bolded terms will help you know what is important. Within the text you will find questions to explore with your Book of Common Prayer, Bible, and 1982 Hymnal. Each chapter presents a question for you to discuss with your parents or another adult in your life. Use these opportunities to become familiar with the books of the church and your family beliefs and practices. Every now and then you'll see a note that begins "Did you know?" I wrote these as little interesting tidbits of information that make reading just a little bit more fun. In the back of the book there is a glossary of new terms and an index. The glossary will help you become familiar with words that are often particular to the Episcopal Church. The index will help you find subjects, people and places that you might need to look up later in class or when you want to refresh your memory at some later date. Keep this book on your shelf for later. Thirty years later, I still have my confirmation book on my shelf!

Here are the things I included to help guide your journey through the book:

Parents and mentors: These are questions for you to explore with your parents or other adults who are important in your life. You might be surprised by the stories that they have to share about their own faith journeys.

Margin notes: These notes define new words, emphasize important concepts in the text, and anticipate questions you might have as a reader. Think of the notes as a little private tutor.

Did you know?: The Christian tradition is filled with fascinating facts. This feature presents some of those interesting facts—the history of words, current practices, or people—that add spice to the main course of the text.

Activities: Every so often, your reading will be interrupted by a question that will send you searching through the Book of Common Prayer, the Bible, or the 1982 Hymnal. These are important texts in the Episcopal Church. According to the church, the Bible contains all things necessary for salvation. It's where we learn about God's saving actions in the world. All three books form our worship together. By searching for the answers to these questions, you'll learn more about the beliefs of the church and you'll have an easier time following the services on Sundays. Answer these questions alone or with a friend. Share your answers in a group. Your youth leader will have the answers to these questions if you want to check out whether you've answered them correctly.

Key terms: These are the words that are bolded in the book. You ought to be familiar with these words and how they are used to describe our faith, tradition, and practices. All the bolded words are defined in the glossary at the back of the book.

Remember, you are responsible for your faith and for your life. Take the opportunity you have been given to learn, question, and explore.

Chapter 1

Baptism and Confirmation: Beginnings

WATERS OF CREATION

Life first began on earth long ago in what scientists call deep time. Nearly three billion years ago, cellular life began in shallow oceans. Two billion years, later life had progressed into multicelled animals visible to the naked eye. Eventually life forms developed that could survive on land. Life originated from water, and life on land still needs water to survive.

People have long recognized the necessity of water in their stories of the beginnings of life. As Christians we share the creation story told by the Israelites, in which God breathed over the face of the waters to call forth all creation. It was from the waters that dry land appeared. It was from the waters that God called swarms of living creatures into being.

Water continued to play a central part in the journeys of the Israelites. It was through the waters of the Red Sea that God led the Israelites out of Egypt and slavery. God provided water for their journey in the desert wilderness. God led the people through the River Jordan into the promised land of Canaan. We read these stories in the **Hebrew Scriptures**, also called the **Old Testament**.

WATERS OF JESUS' BAPTISM

The Gospels of the **Christian Scriptures**, also known as the **New Testament**, tell another story of a watery beginning—the baptism of Jesus. Jesus' baptism began his ministry in the world. At Jesus' baptism in the Jordan River, the heavens parted, the Spirit came down on Jesus, and God said, "You are my Son, the Beloved; with you I am well pleased" (Mark 1:11).

The Gospels tell of Jesus' ministry—proclaiming the coming of the kingdom of God by healing the sick and the lame, inviting the sinners and others who were looked down upon by society to the center of community, and teaching about God's purpose for humankind. Jesus is central to who we are as Christians. Water is part of Jesus' life-giving ministry. At our baptism, in the water, we share in Jesus' baptism, life, death, and resurrection.

WATERS OF BIRTH AND RE-BIRTH

Each of us was conceived in a place rich in water. For nine months we floated in a sea of water inside our mother's womb—first as one cell, then two, then four, then eight. Soon we developed organs and limbs. Finally, one day, we broke through those waters and into the world.

On the day of your baptism, you were born yet again, this time into the body of Christ, the church. Again, you burst forth from water as a new person. Even if you don't remember your own baptism, you've likely seen other people being baptized.

Back on your special day, a priest poured water over your head, or completely plunged you into the water. Now, you didn't re-enter your mother's womb as a man named Nicodemus wondered when he heard Jesus talking about being born again (John 3:1–10). But you *were* born again. You can even think of the baptismal font, the basin that holds the waters of baptism, as a womb in which you were born again. On the day you were baptized, the **Holy Spirit** moved in those waters, making you a new person and giving you spiritual gifts for your life.

Parents and Mentors

Dig out your baptismal and confirmation certificates and other items—such as a baptismal gown, certificate, and candle—related to these two events. When were you baptized? Confirmed? Share what you remember from each.

The waters of baptism are powerful. They are the same waters of *creation* over which God breathed and called forth life. They are the same waters of *freedom* through which God led the Israelites out of a life of slavery in Egypt and the waters of *promise* through which they walked into new life. They are the same waters in which *Jesus* was baptized and the same living water that Jesus offered the Samaritan woman at the well (John 4: 7–15). In these powerful and living waters you were reborn. By those waters you share in the waters of creation, liberation, promise, and new life in Christ. In the waters of baptism you were bathed in the living water where you'll never be thirsty again.

Today's baptisms—unlike the baptism of Jesus in the muddy Jordan River—can be overly sentimental. Babies dressed in white. Receptions with cake and ice cream. Baptisms truly are cause for celebration. But in the festivities we may not notice that a big change is happening before our very eyes. Looking at early Christian baptismal rituals might help us better recognize the change.

Baptism in the Early Church

Baptism meant huge changes in the lives of early Christians. Becoming a Christian sometimes meant putting your life in jeopardy. You'd have to disobey the Roman laws that required you to make sacrifices to the Roman gods, which could easily have gotten you arrested, tried, and even put to death. Some newly baptized Christians, such as those who served in the army, had to give up their jobs. Becoming a Christian in the early centuries after Christ literally meant turning toward a new way of living.

Catechumens began the ritual of baptism by facing west, the direction of the setting sun and the symbolic direction of darkness and evil. They stood on a hair shirt to indicate that they desired to die to their life of sin, then renounced evil three times, professing their desire to give up—virtually die to—their old way of life.

Catechumens are people studying about the Christian faith with the intention of becoming candidates for baptism.

A hair shirt is a shirt made of coarse animal hair worn as an act of penance for one's sins.

The catechumens then turned to the east, the direction of the rising of the sun and the symbolic place of new life, and three times professed their faith in Christ. Then they stepped into a pool of water, submersing their entire bodies. This pool of water symbolized a tomb in which their old selves died and their sins were washed away. It also represented a mother's womb, out of which a new person was born. Finally, stepping up out of the water, they were clothed in a white garment that symbolized their new life in Christ.

Did You Know?

The white alb that bishops, priests, and deacons wear at Eucharist and other church services reminds us of the white dress of baptism.

While we live in a country that doesn't persecute Christians, living as a Christian still means that we see the world differently than others do. So just like early Christians we are expected to act differently than those around us too. We see a world in which God loves all of creation and hopes for a world in which people act in ways that show that they love themselves, one another, and all creation. As new creations in Christ, we are asked to collaborate with God's loving purpose by loving our neighbors, striving for justice, and respecting the dignity of every human being. At our baptism we promise to take these actions and at confirmation we affirm those promises. Just as it was for early Christians, your baptism was the beginning of a new life.

Your Baptism

Your baptism likely took place years ago, long before you could speak or understand what was going on. You might want to take some time with your parents or godparents to talk about your baptism. Ask them to share stories and photographs. Your baptismal certificate will tell you the date of your baptism, the name of the priest who baptized you, and the names of your godparents.

On that day, your parents and godparents presented you to God and the world. They brought you into the **Baptismal Covenant** by making promises on your behalf to believe in God and to follow Christ. They promised to bring you up in the Christian faith. Chapter 6 on **sacraments** explores the Baptismal Covenant in greater detail.

Your baptism was a gift to you by your parents, just as faith is a gift from God. Faith changes how we see the world. The lens of faith in Jesus Christ lets us see the world differently. Instead of a world of random events, we see a world that is part of God's purpose. Instead of a world of unrelated individuals, we see a world of individuals called to be in relationship with one another and whose focus is God and God's son, Jesus Christ. Instead of a world with a creator who is indifferent to the world, we see a world whose creator is in love with and intimately concerned with creation. We can choose to accept or reject that gift of faith. Your confirmation program and this book, along with your knowledge and experience of God, will help you make that choice.

The Baptismal Covenant is God's gift to us. We respond to this gift by following Christ in our words and actions. Covenant is the basis for our relationship with God through Christ.

COVENANT

We've used the word "covenant" a few times in this chapter. It's a word we don't hear very much today. A **covenant** is a particular agreement entered into freely by two or more people, each of whom makes promises to the others in the covenant. Covenants have three characteristics: free choice, promises, and change. As an example, consider marriage. Marriage is a covenant. Two people *freely* choose to be married. As part of their covenant, they *promise* to love, comfort, and be faithful to one another.

And the covenant *changes* each person, too. The bride and groom are still the same people they were before they said "I do," but they have created a new thing—a union of two people. Their covenant makes them act as one. Each agrees to honor their promises—to keep the covenant.

Here's another example. Have you ever babysat or mowed someone's lawn? You promise to provide a particular service and the other person promises to pay you for that service. Your agreement is a covenant. You have freely entered it, the parties made promises, and your actions are changed by the agreement. The difference between this covenant and God's covenant is that the covenant God establishes is a gift and is intended for life. God's covenant shapes our every action and lasts forever.

God offers the covenant to us as a free gift. It is our choice to respond.

Covenant and the Hebrew Scriptures

We learn in the Hebrew Scriptures that God promised that the Israelites would be his people and he would be their God. This was the covenant God established with the people. God required them to be faithful, to treat people fairly, to be merciful, and to be humble before God (Micah 6:8).

As Christians we are part of God's covenant first offered to Abraham and renewed with the Israelites. The history of God's love and salvation as told the Hebrew Scriptures is our history. Our God is the God of Israel who freed the Israelites from slavery in Egypt and led them to the promised land of Canaan. The map on the following page shows one way they may have taken from what is present-day northern Egypt through the Sinai Peninsula and into Israel/Palestine and Jordan. God remained with them through forty years of wandering in the wilderness and provided for their needs—just as God remains with us today and gives us what we need. God is faithful to the covenant and is with us always.

Covenant and the Christian Scriptures

Our God is the God who sent his only Son, Jesus, to live and die as one of us. Through Jesus God renewed his covenant and offered it to all people. In the Christian Scriptures, at the Last Supper Jesus gave us a **New Covenant.** And during the Eucharist every Sunday we remember his words: "Drink from it, all of you; for this is my blood of the covenant, which is poured out for many for the forgiveness of sins" (Matthew 26:27–28). In this New Covenant, Jesus promises to bring us into the

The New Covenant is a new relationship with God through Jesus Christ. This New Covenant was prophesied in Jeremiah 31.

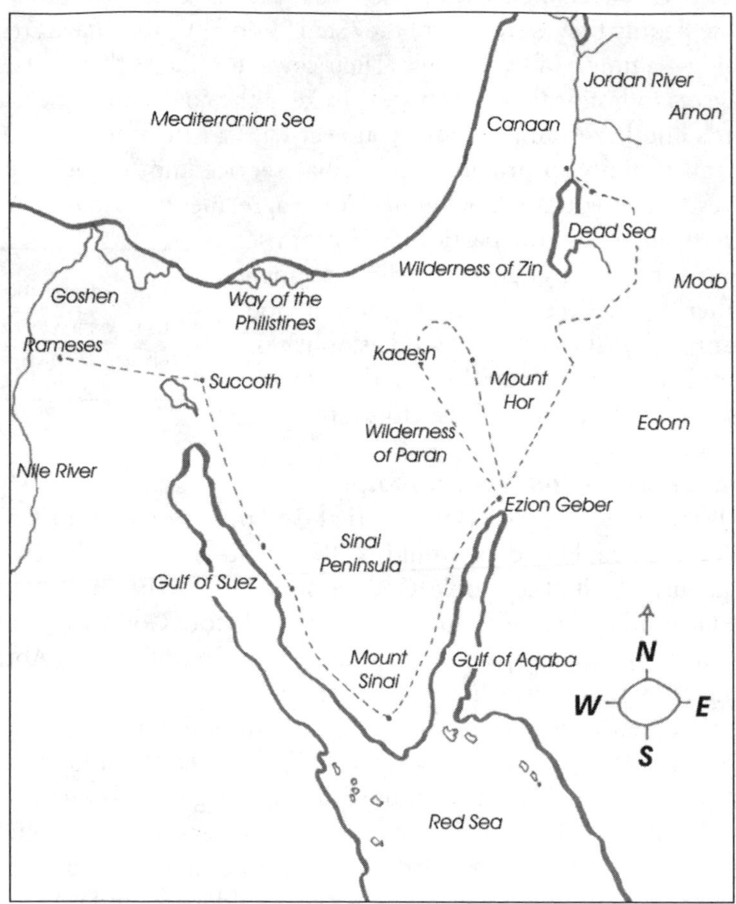

The dotted line on this map of the Ancient Near East shows one way the Israelites may have travelled from slavery in Egypt (far left) to the Promised Land in Canaan (far right).

kingdom of God. Our part of the agreement is to love one another as Jesus has loved us.

Baptismal Covenant

The covenant given by God in the Hebrew Scriptures and in the Christian Scriptures—and our Baptismal Covenant—all share the same basic characteristics: we freely enter, we make promises, and we are changed. If you were baptized as an infant, you might say that you didn't freely choose to be baptized. You'd be right. For you, baptism was a gift, just as being born was a gift. Your parents wanted you to be part of the Christian community—the body of Christ—so they chose for you to be baptized. They spoke on your behalf and promised to teach you about Jesus Christ and what it means to live a Christian life. They stood up in front of family and friends and made it clear that they wanted you to be Christ's own forever!

CONFIRMING THE COVENANT

Now it's your turn. When you're confirmed, you're choosing to renew a covenant with God—to *confirm* the Baptismal Covenant your parents and godparents made on your behalf and you're seeking God's strength to live into that covenant. That's why you're reading this book and participating in your confirmation program—to prepare to renew your belief in God and renew your promises to follow Jesus by the way you act. Confirming your belief and renewing your promises is a serious step. You'll want to know exactly what you're committing yourself to. That's what this book is all about.

Let's start by looking at the confirmation service.

Examination and Presentation

At confirmation the bishop will begin by asking you two questions:

Do you reaffirm your renunciation of evil?
Do you renew your commitment to Jesus Christ?

> These two questions reflect the first six questions you were asked at your baptism. Look on page 302 of the Book of Common Prayer to read those six questions.

Responding with "I do" means you want to turn away from sin and darkness and toward life in Christ. You're saying that you're turning from the values of *sin* and *death* to the values of *God* and *life*. Instead of acting in ways that deny God and break relationships with others, you are saying your actions will honor God and nurture others. The Ten Commandments give us a guideline for right and wrong actions: "Remember the sabbath day" and "honor your father and your mother" are two examples (Exodus 20). Jesus provided a Summary of the Law with this commandment: Love God and love your neighbor as yourself (Matthew 22:37–39). You're promising that your actions will follow God's desire for you. How do we know God's desire? God's desire will be consistent with the Ten Commandments and the Summary of the Law. God's desire will bring life to you, to others, and to your relationships with others.

RENEWING THE PROMISES

Once you've expressed your commitment to follow Christ, the bishop continues by asking the questions of the Baptismal Covenant of you and the whole congregation:

> Do you believe in God the Father?
> Do you believe in Jesus Christ, the Son of God?
> Do you believe in God the Holy Spirit?

If you're going to be confirmed, you'll begin your answer to each of these questions with "I believe." You're already familiar with the complete answers. They make up what we call the Apostles' Creed. In Chapter 4 of this book we'll explore these answers carefully.

The word "creed" comes from the Latin word *credo*—which has the same root as the word for heart. Saying "I believe" isn't just an abstract statement about whether we believe God exists. It's a statement about where our heart is and who will guide our everyday choices. When we stand up at our confirmation and proclaim, "I believe," we're saying that we give our hearts to God. And to give our hearts to God changes how we choose to live.

The questions about how you promise to live are quite specific:

> Will you continue in the apostles' teaching and fellowship, in the breaking of bread, and in the prayers?
>
> Will you persevere in resisting evil, and, whenever you fall into sin, repent and return to the Lord?
>
> Will you proclaim by word and example the Good News of God in Christ?
>
> Will you seek and serve Christ in all persons, loving your neighbor as yourself?
>
> Will you strive for justice and peace among all people, and respect the dignity of every human being?

When you answer "I will, with God's help" to each of these questions, you're promising to take very specific actions throughout your life. You'll be promising to worship regularly, to resist evil, and to ask for forgiveness when you don't live up to your promises. You'll be promising to talk to others about God's love. You'll be promising to love your neighbor as yourself and to strive for justice and peace. Fulfilling these promises is what it means to live into your Baptismal Covenant. Confirmation isn't graduation from church, but an important steppingstone in your faith journey. It's a big "Amen!" to your faith that shows your renewed commitment to Jesus Christ.

Prayers and Blessings

After you've renewed your Baptismal Covenant, the entire congregation will pray to God to give you the strength to fulfill your promises. They'll ask God to deliver you from sin, open your heart with grace and truth, fill you with the Spirit, keep you in faith, and teach you to love others. They'll ask God to send you out into the world to do the good work you've promised to do. Faith, after all, is a relationship with God that we act out in community. Your parents, sponsors, and entire congregation will be there in the church on your confirmation day—and beyond—to help you keep your promises, to stand with you in tough times, to celebrate with you in happy times, and to encourage you to take your faith with you out into the world.

After the prayers, the bishop will lay his hand on you and bless you, asking God to strengthen you with the Holy Spirit, empower you for God's service, and sustain you all the days of your life. The bishop represents the teaching and community of the apostles from the time of Jesus all the way to today and that fellowship throughout the world today. The laying on of hands is the symbolic act that visibly connects you to the apostles and the universal church.

It's Your Choice

At confirmation, you're choosing to renew your Baptismal Covenant. If that's your choice, you're the one who will answer "I do," "I believe," and "I will, with God's help." Your parents and the congregation will continue to support you in your promises. But the choice is entirely yours.

God gives us free choice. Since a covenant is an agreement that we must enter into *freely*, without free choice there wouldn't be a covenant. You can say "no" and walk away from the covenant. Or you can say "yes." No matter what choice you make, however, you'll always be a member of God's household. You were made a member of the household of God at baptism and you'll forever bear the mark of Christ.

This book and your confirmation program will help you understand what these questions mean, guide you about how to keep those promises, and help you decide: Do I turn from evil and toward Jesus? Do I believe in the Trinity? Do I promise to act in the way that follows Jesus? These promises form the backbone of our faith and our relationship with God.

The Trinity is three in one: One God in three persons—the Father, the Son, and the Holy Spirit.

MADE IN THE IMAGE OF GOD AND MARKED AS CHRIST'S OWN FOREVER

If you read the questions you'll be asked at confirmation carefully, you might wonder whether you can, in all honesty, say yes to them. Don't worry. Questioning whether you can promise such faithfulness means you're taking these questions seriously and being honest with yourself. Like all people, you'll fall short of fulfilling them. The **Bible** is filled with people who fall short and struggle with God—from Jacob who wrestled with God in his dreams and Jonah who tried to run away from God in the Hebrew Scriptures, to Peter, the apostle who denied Jesus three times in the Christian Scriptures. God wants us to offer our whole selves—our faith and doubt, our strength and weakness, and our joy and pain. God asks for nothing less than everything.

You Have God

Luckily for us, we aren't alone at confirmation or when we are faced with choices to fulfill our baptismal promises. We have God, Christ, and one another. The service for confirmation recognizes this. Look closely at the response to each question. The answer is: "I will, *with God's help*." God is with you. God has been with you since the beginning and will always be with you to give you the strength to make good choices.

God has given each of us the gifts we need to live a good life. This shouldn't surprise us. From birth we bear the image of God. Genesis tells us that God said, "Let us make humankind in our image, according to our likeness" (Genesis 1:26). People often remark at the likeness of a newborn baby to its parents. "She has her father's eyes," or "He has his mother's nose." Our genetic makeup reflects the DNA of both our mother and father. In that same way, we also reflect the image of our creator, God.

Simply put, like God, we're made to love and to create. We have the abilities to heal broken relationships, to bring justice, to provide for the physical and mental well-being of others, and even to create new life—both physically by creating new families and spiritually by sharing our faith with others. God has given us the ability to live into the baptismal promises we commit to at our confirmation.

Now, it would be unrealistic to end the conversation there. Yes, we're made to do good, but we sometimes choose to do bad things. We ignore God and think only of ourselves. We forget the goodness of God that's in us. We harm ourselves and others. We fall short of our promises. It's a given.

You Have Christ

Knowing that we'll fall short of the mark, one of the promises we make is that *whenever* we fall into sin, we'll repent and return to the Lord. Notice that we don't say *if* we fall into sin. Falling into sin is certain. But when that happens, God will forgive us and set our hearts right again and again. All we promise to do is to ask for God's forgiveness and guidance.

God loved us so much he gave his only son, Jesus, to redeem, or save, us. Jesus carried our sins on the cross and was raised from the dead. Today, we share in Jesus' resurrection and in the new life he offers us. In the waters of baptism we were cleansed from sin and came out of the waters a new creation in Christ. At baptism the priest also marked our foreheads with the sign of the cross, sealing us by the Holy Spirit and marking us as Christ's own forever. The cross represents Jesus' sacrifice that brought us freedom from sin and the promise of eternal life. The cross means that no matter what we do, we don't have the final say.

> God, Jesus Christ, and our faith community help us keep our baptismal promises.

You Have Community

Your community—the rest of the church, the household of God—will help you keep your promises. Belief in God, and therefore baptism and confirmation, are not private matters. At confirmation, the entire congregation witnesses your vows and promises. They promise in turn to do all in their power to support you in your life in Christ. These are the people with whom you worship, study, pray, and do service. These are the people with whom you say "We believe" as you begin the Nicene Creed each Sunday. When your belief falters, they will believe for you. At your confirmation, the entire congregation joins you in renewing their own Baptismal Covenant.

HOW WILL READING THIS BOOK HELP?

Preparing for confirmation is an opportunity to learn about what it means to follow Jesus Christ, to believe in a triune God—God as Father, Son, and Holy Spirit—and to live according to our baptismal promises. This book was written to help you explore these beliefs and promises. You can choose to take the promises made at your baptism as your own or reject them. Without this freedom, covenant has no meaning. Even if you decide to reject the promises, however, you'll always be a member of the Christian family. Baptism is a once-and-for-all initiation into the body of Christ. Just as you'll always bear the DNA of your parents, no matter where you go or how far from home you travel, you'll always be a member of the body of Christ and bear the image of God.

You're facing a pretty big decision. Saying that you'll renounce evil and follow Jesus, that you believe in God, and that you promise to live into that belief with specific actions is big stuff. You'll want to be ready. If you're to claim your faith, you must actively seek to understand God, yourself, and your relationship with God. That's what this book and your confirmation program will help you do. You'll learn about Jesus and God, the language of worship, belief, church structure, and sacraments, so that you can share your belief and practices with others and participate in worship at your own church. You'll explore how to read and think about the Bible so that you can hear what God is saying today. You'll learn about **prayer** so that you can deepen your relationship with God. You'll learn about **ministry** (a call each of us receives from God to serve) and discover methods to discern your own ministry in the world.

It is your responsibility to be ready to claim your faith. Take time to learn about God, Jesus, and the language and practice of your faith.

Each chapter has activities that will help you connect what you're reading to the Bible, the Book of Common Prayer, and your own experiences. The Bible tells about God, Jesus, and ourselves. The Book of Common Prayer defines our worship as a community. Our experiences as a community are where God meets us and reveals himself to us.

Each chapter also has questions to explore with a parent or mentor. Talk about them together. They're a way to share your journey with people who care about you. Your community was with you at your baptism and welcomed you into the church. Your church community will support you in this next step to becoming a more active part of it. Take advantage of the wealth of their experience and knowledge. Often, other people can reveal to us a different perspective on God, opening new visions for us as well.

You've probably already noticed comments in the margins of the text. These comments will help guide your reading. Sometimes church vocabulary can be hard to understand. Don't let the words get in the way. The rich images, rituals, and words that express our understanding of God and the world are sometimes necessarily complex. God is ultimately a mystery, beyond knowing. Still, we use our senses—sight, touch, hearing, taste, and smell—to express that mystery. Any one way falls a little bit short because God is in all things and beyond our capacity to know or describe. Ultimately we may agree with the thirteenth-century monk Meister Eckhart, who said, "nothing is so like God as silence."

A JOURNEY WITH GOD

Baptism is only the beginning of a life with Christ. Being a Christian is a journey that never ends. God continually yearns to be close to us and continually yearns for a restored relationship with all people. At confirmation we make a mature and public affirmation of our faith and recommit ourselves to the promises we made, or were made on our behalf, at baptism. We say, "yes," to God—to God's yearning for us and making a difference in our lives. Confirmation is part of our Christian journey. We hope that through your preparation for confirmation you will continue your journey with God and claim your full membership in the church.

Chapter 2

The Bible: Stories about Yesterday, Today, and Tomorrow

When I turned eighteen, my parents gave me a photo album. Page one shows my certificate of birth, stating the exact time and place of my birth, followed by my footprints, identifying me as a unique person. The pages are filled with people and places: relatives and friends, special gatherings, important events, and family trips. I take this book out again and again. Each time, I remember something different about the stories—they change because I have changed. One photograph shows the four-room house in Pine Bluff, Arkansas, that my parents brought me home to from the hospital. We were the only white family living in an all-black neighborhood. My father was teaching at A.M.&M. College, a black college now a part of the University of Arkansas, as part of his commitment to the Civil Rights Movement. When I was younger and heard these stories, I was amazed at how small our house was and the fact that I slept in a dresser-drawer instead of a crib. As I grew older, I began to see these pictures differently. I asked my parents about the hardships they endured to remain committed to civil rights. I asked about the marches they walked. My amazement turned to commitment. Their commitment to social justice and respect for all people became my commitment.

The more I look at this album, the more clearly it speaks of who my family is and who I am. Social justice is woven throughout my life. I chose to major in economics in college to understand how economic policies affect the poor and underprivileged. Today, I volunteer my time tutoring young people from low-income families. My husband, two children, and I take time as a family to serve at soup kitchens. The album reveals other themes as well. I see my love of low-budget travel in photographs of camping trips through Europe. I see how important God and my faith community is in my life from pictures of my baptism at age nine, of trips with youth groups, and of our church's inner-city summer camp where I worked as a counselor and director. These stories began when I was a baby barely conscious of my surroundings. Retelling these stories deepens the knowledge of who I am and my commitment to social justice and to my church.

Parents and Mentors

Share family photographs and tell some of your own stories from childhood. What are some of your best memories? How do they affect you today?

The Bible is like a family album. It too is a collection of picture stories. The primary characters are God and God's people. The Bible tells the stories of God's people and God's actions throughout history beginning with the creation of the world. Through the stories we see long threads of common traditions, identities, and God's enduring love of creation. The stories in the Bible are very human, filled with love, family, and faithfulness as well as deceit, murder, greed, and power. And they are stories of God's abiding love and offer of forgiveness. They're stories of the human family living in the grace of God.

The Hebrew Scriptures teach us about God and his relationship with his chosen people, the Israelites. God begins this relationship with a covenant in which he promises to guide his people, provide for them, and love them. In turn, the Israelites promise to worship God and live by God's laws. The Hebrew Scriptures are made up of stories, laws, poetry, and history about God's steadfast love. The Christian Scriptures continue the story of God's love and covenant. They tell of God's greatest act of love—coming into the world as a person, Jesus, who shows us what it means to love God, ourselves, and our neighbor. The ultimate act of love happened when Jesus suffered and died for us on the cross. On the third day, God raised him from the dead, opening the way for us also to give up our sins and share in new life. God entered our history as a human to deliver us from the sin that separates us from God.

A covenant is an agreement entered into freely by two or more parties. It is through a covenant that God established a relationship with the Israelites. He promised to be their God and they promised to be his people.

Even if we read the Bible from cover to cover, we're never really finished reading it. Each time we return to the Bible—the family album of the people of God—we don't just remember, we relive the events and are changed by them. We learn more about ourselves and our God.

Activity: Read the collect for Proper 28 found on page 236 of the Book of Common Prayer. According to this prayer, why do we read the Bible?

A LIBRARY OF BOOKS

The word "bible" comes from the Greek word *biblios*, meaning book. Although today the Bible is generally bound into a single volume, it's not just one book, but a library of sixty-six books of the Christian and Hebrew Scriptures and a few additional books called the Apocrypha. Recognizing the Bible as a library helps us to know how to read it. First of all, just as we don't take the first book off the shelf in a library, we don't begin reading the Bible with page one and continue to the end. Generally, we choose a book from among many books based on what we're interested in or what question we want to explore. Secondly, just as a library contains many different kinds of books, the books of the Bible are also examples of many types of literature. The Bible includes histories, sermons, legal documents, poetry, hymns, romances, stories of intrigue, and letters. Because each is written for a different purpose, we read them differently.

> The Bible, like a library, is a collection of different kinds of books, written by a variety of authors over a long period of time.

The Testaments (or Covenants)

The Bible has two major parts—the Hebrew Scriptures, or the Old Testament, and the Christian Scriptures, or the New Testament. But "testament" isn't a very accurate word. Although Old and New Testaments do *testify* to, or show, the ways God has saved his people throughout history, the word "testament," as it's used in the Bible, really means covenant. We call the Old and New Covenants "Old Testament" and "New Testament" because years and years ago, the people who translated the Bible from Greek into Latin used the wrong word. If you're learning a foreign language in school, you know how easy that is to do!

In this book, we'll refer to the Old Testament as the *Hebrew Scriptures* and the New Testament as the *Christian Scriptures*. By using the words "Hebrew Scriptures," we are recognizing that these writings are the sacred stories of the Israelites, most of which were written in Hebrew. These sacred stories are also our sacred stories. No one so far has agreed on a good parallel term to replace "New Testament." The words "Christian Scriptures" highlight the fact that the New Testament is made up of writings of the early communities that followed Jesus.

The **Hebrew Scriptures** tell the stories of the Israelites and their covenant relationship with God. In this covenant, God promises to be with the chosen people, strengthen them, and encourage them. The people, in return, promise to keep God's law. The **Christian Scriptures** tell how God renewed and strengthened the covenant by entering the world as a human being named Jesus. Jesus suffered a painful death as a human on the cross and was resurrected. His life, death, and resurrection give us a new way to know that keeping God's law is the best way to respond to the love God has freely given to us.

Activity: Read about the New Covenant in the Catechism on page 850 of the Book of Common Prayer. What is the New Covenant? What did the Messiah promise? What response did Christ require?

ORIGINS OF THE BIBLE

The Bible was written over a period of about eleven hundred years—from about 1,000 B.C.E. to about 100 C.E., by many authors, editors, and communities of the ancient Near East, a region of the world we today call the Middle East, which includes the modern-day countries of Egypt, Palestine, Israel, Jordan, Syria, and Lebanon, as shown in the map on the next page. The earliest writings began as songs and stories the people sang and told when they all gathered together in their homes and at religious festivals. Parents passed these stories to their children from generation to generation and formed a shared memory of their community. These stories told each generation who they were. The stories also helped them make choices that determined their future. The Israelites knew that they were descendants of Abraham, whom God promised would be the father of a great nation. They knew that they belonged to a community that upheld the law that Moses gave. They knew that God was on their side.

It's much like the stories we share at family gatherings. Telling and retelling the stories of a great-grandma who served her city as mayor helps a family remember and pass along its sense of civic duty. Knowing this history may inspire

Christians and Jews share the books of the Hebrew Scriptures as the word of God. What Christians commonly call the Hebrew Scriptures, Jews call the *Tanakh*. Muslims also accept some of the books of the Hebrew Scriptures and the Gospels of the Christian Scripture as holy writings.

B.C.E., or "Before the Common Era," is the modern designation for the years before the birth of Christ and replaces "B.C." C.E., or "Common Era," refers to the years *after* the birth of Christ and replaces "A.D."

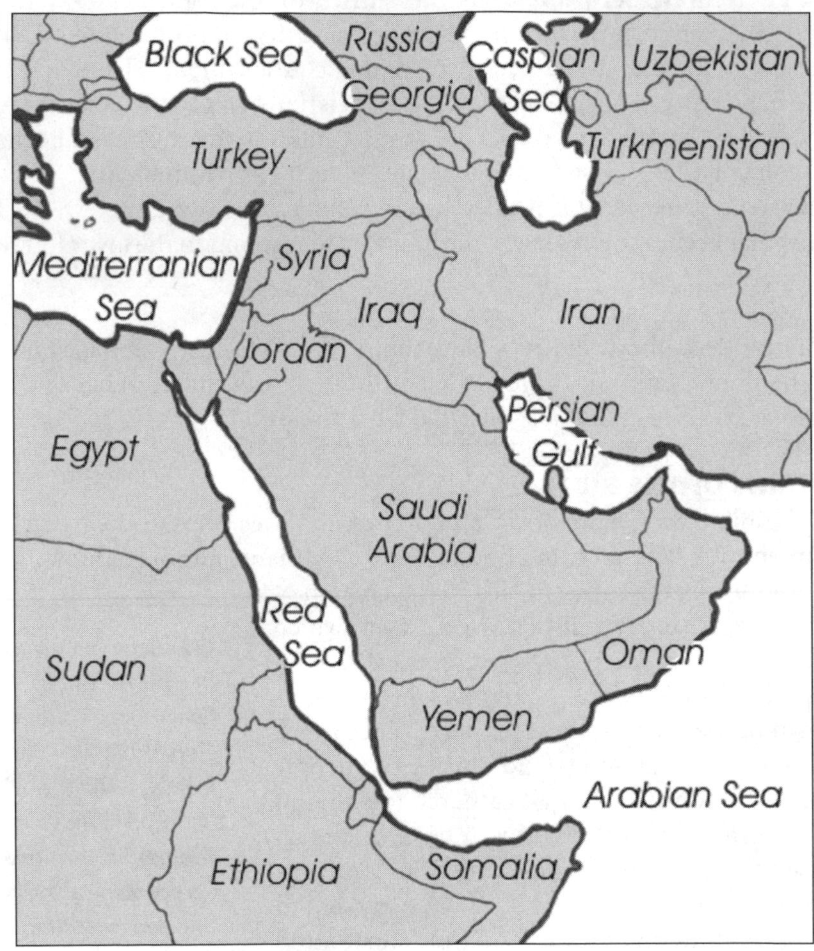

This map shows the modern-day nations of the Middle East. This is the geographic area of the Ancient Near East—the land of the people in the Bible.

future generations in the family to share in a commitment to public service. Every family will have a different identity and different stories.

Although many of the stories in the Bible tell of people and events, the stories weren't necessarily intended to relate a record of "actual events." They were meant to address basic questions of existence such as "Who are we?" and "What is the purpose of our life together?" The Israelite storytellers were sharing and celebrating the community's main identity—as the people God chose, and to whom he promised land. The storytellers were helping their listeners remember that they were God's chosen people, and were expected to live in a way that preserved their friendship with one another and with God, by keeping God's law. In lots of different ways, and through many, many characters, the stories help explore this really important question: "What does it mean to say we are the people of God?"

For example, let's look at the creation stories. They're not meant to be a scientific description of how and when the world was created. They express a people's understanding of God and God's relationship to the world. God is an intimate and divine ruler of all creation and the source of all blessings. God created heaven and earth. God created night and day. God created living creatures. God created humankind in his image. And throughout the first creation story (Genesis 1:1–2:3), we hear the refrain, "And God saw that it was good." This is a world that is ordered by the Divine and is good.

Did You Know?

The book of Genesis has two creation stories. One begins with Genesis 1:1 and another begins with Genesis 2:4.

Hebrew Scriptures

The oldest books in the Bible are in the Hebrew Scriptures. As the Hebrew language developed into written word, scribes began to write the stories on papyrus scrolls. The basics for the story of how the Israelites were led by Moses out of slavery in Egypt to their rise as an independent nation in Canaan, for example, is believed to have been written in the tenth century B.C.E.—a thousand years before the birth of Christ—by a poet hired by King Solomon. The poet did his work by hand—after all, the printing press wouldn't be invented for more than two thousand years!—so few copies would have been made. The stories were passed down from generation to generation by telling these stories aloud at special meals and community worship.

Papyrus was made from long strips of papyrus reeds that grew on the banks of the Nile. Sheets were joined together into rolls up to a hundred feet long, though the average biblical scroll was twenty to twenty-six feet long.

More than one written tradition developed, each explaining past events in different ways, for different cultures and different circumstances. Writers of ancient sacred texts followed a rule of not deleting anything that had already been accepted as sacred writing, but they could add material. Scribes would insert contemporary ideas and practices into earlier stories, giving historical authority to current understandings and practices.

Ancient editors collected, adapted, and reinterpreted the collective stories in light of their communities' experiences. The result was not a single, clear account of a community's history and laws, but a set of stories that sometimes repeat previous accounts and sometimes even contradict one another. The intention of the editors wasn't to present one single perspective, but to preserve the variety of viewpoints of sacred literature. This editing likely occurred over a long period of time, but was mostly complete by the sixth century B.C.E.

The Hebrew Scriptures are thought to have been written between the tenth and fifth centuries.

The canon is a set of writings that are officially accepted by a community as Holy Scripture.

By the first century C.E., Israelite communities recognized a common set of texts as the official Hebrew Scriptures and the Word of God. These texts became the **canon** (the collection of books officially accepted as Holy Scripture) because they were the central texts of the Israelite community. The Hebrew Scripture was the Bible for the Israelites at the time of Jesus and also in large part later for early Christian communities. The Jewish and Christian canons of the Hebrew Scriptures are similar, but not identical. For example, the Roman Catholic canon (also recognized by the Episcopal Church) includes writings in the Hebrew Scripture that are not part of the Hebrew canon. The Hebrew canon has not changed since the first century C.E. and the Christian canon has not changed since the sixteenth century C.E.

Christian Scriptures

The Christian Scriptures developed a lot differently than the Hebrew Scriptures. First of all, the texts of the New Testament were written over a much shorter period—only about a hundred years—and they were written in *koine*, the common Greek that was spoken in the Roman Empire during the first century. Like the early writings in the Hebrew Scriptures, at first, news of Jesus' life, ministry, and resurrection spread by word of mouth. Early Christians believed that Jesus would return at any moment, and the reign of God was about to begin, so it didn't seem necessary to write down the story of Jesus for future generations.

The earliest parts of the Christian Scriptures were letters written by the Apostle Paul to various Christian communities he visited, addressing the problems they faced and encouraging their new faith. These letters, written in Greek, were delivered by a messenger who read the letters aloud to the community. Paul's letters were among the earliest writings circulated among Christian communities. The earliest letter is 1 Thessalonians, believed to have been written in about 50 C.E., not quite twenty years after the crucifixion of Jesus.

Activity: Read 1 Thessalonians 1:1–3 and Corinthians 1:1–3. How do these beginnings remind you of a modern letter?

Scholars believe that the earliest of the four gospels, the book of Mark, was written about thirty years after Jesus' death and resurrection. Next came the Gospels of Matthew and Luke, both written sometime in the second half of the first century. It's likely that the writers of Matthew and Luke were familiar with the Gospel according to Mark, as well as a third text that no longer exists but that scholars think probably contained sayings of Jesus.

The last gospel to be written was the Gospel according to John, probably completed in the last part of the first century.

All four gospels tell the story of Jesus' life and ministry, but disagree about the details. That's because the authors had different thoughts about exactly who Jesus was, and they wrote for different audiences. Mark, for instance, ends the story with the empty tomb on Easter morning, while the other gospels tell about the many times Jesus appeared after his resurrection.

Christian writings first circulated as codexes, folded sheets of paper stitched together and covered into notebooks. Codexes differentiated Christian from Hebrew writings, which were on scrolls. Christian communities favored codexes also because more text could be bound into a codex. Our familiar bound Bible didn't exist until the European-style printing press was invented in Germany in the sixteenth century. As the stories, liturgies, hymns, and letters of the Christian community were circulated and used in worship, a common set of writings began to emerge. By the end of the fourth century, the church determined which writings should be included in the Holy Scriptures. That is, the Christian biblical canon was set. In the sixteenth century, another Roman Catholic Church council added additional writings—the Apocrypha—which are commonly placed between the Hebrew and Christian Scriptures. While the Episcopal Church and the Roman Catholic Church recognize the Apocrypha as a second canon, Protestant churches don't.

A VARIETY OF FORMS OF LITERATURE

As we've mentioned earlier, the Bible is made up of a variety of types of literature—laws, history, fiction, hymns, romances, letters, and so on. Here's a look at some of the kinds, or genres, of literature we find in the Bible.

Law. The **Pentateuch**, the first five books of the Hebrew Scriptures, is a combination of laws and history. We've already talked a little about history. The law, or *torah*, is the code by which people lived and determined community worship, daily living patterns, moral behavior, and business ethics. The laws with which you are most likely familiar are the Ten Commandments, the covenant law delivered by Moses. But these aren't the only laws in the Pentateuch. There are laws about how land is inherited, what to eat, and how to treat criminals. These laws were written for a particular time and don't always apply to the way we live today. Indeed, because the Pentateuch includes laws from a variety of time periods, they sometimes contradict one another.

The law of the covenant is much more than the Ten Commandments given by God to Moses. In fact, the Hebrew word for law is "torah," which also is the word for the first five books of the Hebrew Bible.

Poetry. Examples of poetry in the Bible are Psalms, Proverbs, Isaiah, and Song of Songs. This poetry tells of love and life (Song of Songs), provides moral instruction (Proverbs), and provides the hymns for worship (Psalms).

Fiction. Some books are meant to be works of literary fiction. Just like today's fiction, these books aren't meant to convey actual events. Trying to determine whether the events in the book could have actually happened misses the point of fiction. They were meant to be read for pleasure, or to learn a moral or truth. A modern example is the story of George Washington cutting down the cherry tree. Whether he actually cut down the tree is not important. What is important is the truth of George Washington's character: he was an honest man. Most scholars agree that Jonah, for example, was intended as a fictional story. Whether Jonah could actually survive being swallowed by a great fish is irrelevant. The author intended to tell a compelling story that would teach the reader that God is merciful, even to those who don't deserve mercy.

Prophecy. Much of the prophetic books (Isaiah, Hosea, and Micah, for example) are speeches given by a prophet to an audience to teach them how to live good lives.

Although the word "prophecy" today refers to predicting a future event, prophecy in terms of the Bible refers to writings or sayings that reveal God's will.

Letters. We call the letters in the Christian Scriptures epistles. The **Epistles** are letters that Paul and the other apostles wrote to the communities they had visited, to help them address their problems and concerns. It's easy to see that these are letters by their opening words—they begin with words like "Dear So-and-So," just as we begin our letters and emails today. Paul's letters to Corinth, a town in Greece, for example, begin: "To the Church of God that is in Corinth . . . Grace to you." The letters are half of a complete conversation, making them sometimes difficult to understand. It's like listening to one end of a telephone conversation. Sometimes we have to guess what questions Paul was answering.

It's important to keep in mind the kind of literature you're reading in the Bible. Just as you wouldn't read a telephone book for spiritual inspiration, you wouldn't read the laws in Leviticus the same way you'd read the hymns in Psalms or the history in Exodus. The laws in Leviticus are literally legal codes that governed behavior for a particular people at a particular time, while the hymns in Psalms appeal more universally to human experiences such as joy, pain, sorrow, and forgiveness.

UNITY OF THE BIBLE

The Bible's various origins and many kinds of literature might make you wonder what keeps them together. The unity of the Bible can be understood in the **shema**, the Hebrew declaration of faith in one God:

> *Hear, O Israel: The LORD is our God, the LORD alone.*
> (Deuteronomy 6:4)

This is the prayer that devout Jewish people say every day. It reminds them, as the many books of the Bible remind us all, that the Lord is our God. The Bible is an important way we hear that the Lord is our God. The Bible is the result of the interaction between human beings and the divine. The storytellers, writers, and editors were inspired to know—and to share with others—that God enters human history to care for his people and tell us his will. It's through the Bible that God speaks to us.

The Bible is a witness to the Lord our God. God is the source of all life, and creation bears God's divine imprint. God is one who speaks first in creation and later leads, directs, forgives, judges, and is also the end of all things. Jesus is the way God reveals himself to us as a human being. In the Bible we find common themes of creation, sin, judgment, redemption, and restoration. The stories of the Bible tell the events of human history moving to fulfill God's purpose.

To witness is to tell others what you have seen and heard.

Activity: Find the section "The Holy Scriptures" in the Catechism found in the Book of Common Prayer. What helps us to interpret the meaning of the Bible?

A TOUR OF THE BIBLE

With that broad introduction, let's take a closer tour of the Bible.

Hebrew Scriptures

The Hebrew Scriptures is composed of four major divisions—the Pentateuch (Torah), the Historical Books, the Poetical and Wisdom Books, and the Prophetic Books. Here are the names of all thirty-nine books.

The Hebrew Scriptures

Pentateuch (Torah)

Genesis
Exodus
Leviticus
Numbers
Deuteronomy

The Historical Books

Joshua
Judges
Ruth
1, 2 Samuel
1, 2 Kings
1, 2 Chronicles
Ezra
Nehemiah
Esther

The Poetical and Wisdom Books

Job
Psalms
Proverbs
Ecclesiastes
Song of Solomon

The Prophetic Books

Isaiah
Jeremiah
Lamentations
Ezekiel
Jonah
Micah
Nahum
Habakkuk

Daniel	Zephaniah
Hosea	Haggai
Joel	Zechariah
Amos	Malachi
Obadiah	

Note: The Hebrew Bible arranges these books differently. For the most part, however, the books and their contents are the same.

The Pentateuch (Torah)

The first five books of the Bible are known as the Pentateuch.

> The word "Pentateuch" comes from two Greek words—*penta* meaning "five" and *tecuhoi* meaning "books."

The first eleven chapters of Genesis, the first book of the Bible, tell about the beginnings of humanity—from the creation of the world and the first humans, to the fall of Adam and Eve, the Great Flood, and the scattering of people into different nations with different languages (the tower of Babel). These early narratives, or stories, expressed basic beliefs about the origin of the world and the nature of humans, and explained why there are different kinds of people in the world. After the story of the tower of Babel, the particular story of God's chosen people begins. It starts with the birth of Abraham, the one to whom God promised land and many descendants. Abraham became the father of the people of God.

The Jewish people call these books the Torah, the Hebrew word for law or teaching. These books contain the law of Moses (including the Ten Commandments) and legal codes, as well as the central story of God's chosen people, the nation of Israel, from the covenant established with Abraham, to the liberation of the Israelites from Egypt, to the giving of the Ten Commandments, to the journey in the wilderness, to the death of Moses. A central theme of the Pentateuch is the covenant relationship between God and his people. Together, the laws and the narratives teach the people ethical living and help them understand their relationship with God.

The Historical Books

The historical books also contain a variety of types of literature. The historical narratives in Joshua, Judges, 1 and 2 Samuel, and 1 and 2 Kings tell the continuous history of Israel from the end of Moses' life to the exile of the Israelites in Assyria and Babylon a thousand years later in the 500s B.C.E. Dates, particularly those for the stories of ancient Israel including the flight from Egypt and Moses, are difficult to pin down. Central actions in this history are the conquest of the land by Joshua and the building of the Temple by King Solomon as a place to keep the Ark of the Covenant, a chest that contained the Ten Commandments and was believed to represent God's presence among the people. During this time Israel was governed first by judges and then by kings. It faced continual threats from invaders and at one time the kingdom divided into the Northern Kingdom (Israel) and the Southern Kingdom (Judah). Ezra and Nehemiah tell about the return of the Israelites from exile in Babylon. Ruth and Esther are believed to be historical fictions written to teach important lessons to the community. Ruth teaches about the importance of hospitality toward foreigners, while Esther tells how the oppressed must be persistent to be treated fairly. The historical books are rich with individual characters whose stories teach us about sin and redemption and about God's steadfast love for his people.

The Ark of the Covenant was a chest holding the Ten Commandments.

Poetic Books and Books of Wisdom

The five books in this category contain a greater diversity of literature than other divisions in the Hebrew Scriptures. Job, Proverbs, and Ecclesiastes are known as wisdom literature. Unlike other books in the Hebrew Scriptures, they don't focus on the details of the nation of Israel. Instead, they address individual concerns of maintaining right relationships that will lead to success and the approval of God. Proverbs addresses moral life with warnings that tell the consequences of our behavior. An example is: "Do not boast about tomorrow, for you do not know what a day may bring" (Proverbs 27:1). Through the tale of the suffering of a righteous man, the book of Job addresses the question of whether bad behavior results in human suffering, while Ecclesiastes considers suffering and joy as part of a natural cycle of existence: "For everything there is a season" (Ecclesiastes 3:1).

Psalms and the Song of Solomon are books of poetry. Psalms are prayers sung at Temple worship. Psalms express an array of human emotion—from praise to sorrow to anger. The Song of Solomon is poetry that celebrates human love.

Activity: What book of the Bible is included in its entirety in the Book of Common Prayer?

The Prophetic Books

The prophetic books are comprised mostly of long speeches that prophets gave to a live audience, which were later written down either by the prophet or one of his associates. As with other biblical writings, later authors added biographies of the prophets, edited, and added to the original statements in the book.

The age of prophets began with the rise of kings and ended during the return of the people from Babylonian exile in 538 B.C.E. Prophets, holy men and women of wisdom and vision, were called by God to play a unique role as the people's spokesperson to God and God's messenger to the people. Prophets criticized rich and powerful people, and urged them to help the poor and helpless. Prophets supported social justice; prophets brought God's word to the people ("Thus says the Lord") that often condemned current practices against God's will. At the same time, prophets took the side of the people and begged God for mercy and forgiveness. The prophetic books bring the books of the Hebrew Scriptures to a close.

A prophet is a person who communicated with God. Sometimes prophets spoke to the people on behalf of God and at other times prophets spoke to God for the people. Elijah was a prophet.

Christian Scriptures

The Christian Scriptures are composed of twenty-seven books divided into four categories—the Gospels, history, Epistles and the apocalyptic literature. These books were chosen by early Church councils from among a wide range of early Christian literature based on their consistency with the teachings of the apostles, the tradition of narratives of Jesus' life and ministry, and the accepted literature of Christian communities. As we noted above, Paul's letters predate the Gospels, so as you can see, the books don't appear in the order in which they were written.

The table lists the books of the Christian Scriptures and their divisions.

THE CHRISTIAN SCRIPTURES

Gospels

Matthew	Luke
Mark	John

History

The Acts of the Apostles

Epistles

Romans
1, 2 Corinthians
Galatians
Ephesians
Philippians
Hebrews
James
1, 2 Peter
Colossians
1, 2 Thessalonians
1, 2 Timothy
Titus
Philemon
1, 2, 3 John
Jude

Apocalyptic

The Revelation to John

The Gospels

The Gospels—Matthew, Mark, Luke, and John—proclaim the *good news* of salvation through Jesus Christ by telling about Jesus' life and teachings. At the time the gospels were written the word gospel meant an announcement of a happy event such as the birth of a son or a marriage. So the Gospel according to Mark begins, "The beginning of the good news (gospel) of Jesus Christ, the son of God."

The word "gospel" means "good news."

Matthew, Mark, and Luke repeat the stories and sayings of Jesus almost identically. Because of their similar point of view, they are called the *Synoptic* Gospels. Each, however, emphasizes different aspects of Jesus' life and teaching. Matthew presents Jesus as a great teacher and emphasizes the authority and wisdom with which Jesus interpreted Jewish law; Mark presents Jesus in terms of the great prophets of the Hebrew Scriptures—Elijah, Moses, and Jeremiah; Luke presents Jesus as the savior for all people and emphasizes his royal heritage as a descendant of the celebrated King David.

The Gospel according to John, the last gospel to be written, is much different than the other three gospels in terms of the timeline and the details of Jesus' life. This gospel emphasizes the divinity of Jesus—the teaching that

These are the traditional symbols of the four evangelists. Saint Matthew the Evangelist is the "Divine Man." Saint Mark the Evangelist is a winged lion for royalty. Saint Luke the Evangelist is the winged ox for the sacrifice of Jesus. Saint John the Evangelist is a rising eagle.

Jesus is God—to a much greater extent than do the Synoptic Gospels.

"Synoptic" means to see from the same point of view.

Throughout the gospels are sayings of Jesus, including parables, details of Jesus' life, and hymns used by early Christian communities. **Parables**, stories used as metaphors for teaching, appear in the Synoptic Gospels. Examples are the parables of the kingdom of God in Matthew where Jesus tells the disciples that the kingdom of God is like a treasure hidden in a field, like a mustard seed, and like yeast. Because parables teach with comparisons, or metaphors, we can understand them by calling to mind our own experiences. For example, to understand the parable of the lost coins (Luke 15:8–10), we must think about our own experience of losing something and finding it. Parables invite our thoughts and feelings, so even today they're living instruments of instruction for us.

Activity: Which of the four gospels tell the story of Jesus' birth? Which of the four gospels begins from the earliest point in time?

Acts of the Apostles

Acts is the story of the birth and growth of the church from the time Jesus returned to heaven until the Apostle Paul arrived in Rome. It's a sequel to the Gospel according to Luke—scholars think it was written by the same author. Acts tells us about how the early church began and Christianity spread and addressed problems the early church faced. A central figure in Acts is the Apostle Paul, a Jew who grew up in the Greek city of Tarsus. Paul experienced a dramatic vision of Jesus, converted to Christianity, and dedicated his life to establishing and guiding Christian communities. Two central themes of Acts are that the church continues the history of Israel and that gentiles, or non-Israelites, are welome into Christian communities and can share God's promise of salvation. By portraying the expansion of the early church as being led by the Holy Spirit, Acts gives early Christians the confidence that communities are living and growing according to God's will.

The word "epistle" comes from the Greek word *epistolos*, meaning letter.

The Epistles

The Epistles are a set of twenty-one letters or writings in the form of letters. Thirteen are written either by the Apostle Paul or by one of his followers in Paul's name. Paul's letters (except Romans) were sent to early Christian communities he had established during mission journeys throughout the eastern part of the Mediterranean to provide them with continued guidance. The map shows these communities.

Letters were a common way for leaders of various church communities to communicate. They address issues such as leadership and gifts for ministry, as well as questions such as when the Messiah—Jesus, the Savior promised by God—would return and whether Gentiles had to follow Jewish law to join the Christian community. The letters show how God continued to work in the early church through the Holy Spirit.

Reading the epistles can be like listening to one end of a telephone conversation. We know one side of the conversation from the letters that we have in the Bible, but we don't have the letters that asked the questions or posed the problems in the first place. We sometimes have to

The map of the Mediterranean shows major communities where Paul travelled.

guess what the initial problem or question was as well as the details of the particular issue.

The Revelation to John

The Revelation to John is a vision of the end of the world. It's called **apocalyptic** (Greek for "reveals") because it reveals something that is unknown. Most scholars do not believe that it was written to predict future events. It's filled with hymns, gruesome language, war, and bloodshed, which isn't surprising if you know that at the time it was written the world was hostile to Christians, and acknowledging that you were a Christian could lead to your death. With a lot of complicated symbolism, the author of the Revelation to John comforts faithful Christians and assures them that God will punish those who persecute them. This book is perhaps one of the most difficult books of the Bible to understand.

> Apocalyptic writings tell something that has been revealed.

American readers today have become fascinated with the Revelation to John as portrayed in the modern apocalyptic-fiction series *Left Behind.* Novels about the end times aren't new to American literature. Your parents might remember *666*, written in 1970. *In the Twinkling of an Eye* and *The Mark of the Beast*, two other apocalyptic novels, were written in the early

1900s. They're fun to read, but they are not accurate portrayals of the Revelation to John.

The Apocrypha

The thirty-nine books of the Hebrew Scriptures and twenty-seven books of the Christian Scriptures comprise the sixty-six books of the Bible. In addition to those books, the Episcopal Church (along with the Roman Catholic Church) also recognizes the following deuterocanonical writings as Holy Scripture:

Deuterocanonical

Tobit
Judith
Esther (additions)
Wisdom of Solomon
Sirach (Ecclesiasticus)
Baruch
1–4 Maccabees
Daniel (additions)

These additional books are known as **Apocrypha**, meaning "unseen," or *deutero-canonical*, meaning "second canon." They were added to the Christian canon in the sixteenth century, about twelve hundred years after the first Christian canon was established. These additional books, generally located between the Hebrew and Christian Scriptures, are literature found in either the ancient Greek translation of the Hebrew Scriptures called the Septuagint, or in Latin translations of the Greek, but are not contained in the Hebrew canonical text. In the sixteenth century, the Roman Catholic Church accepted them into the canons of Scripture and the Church of England followed suit. Most Protestant churches do not recognize deuterocanonical literature as Holy Scripture. The Apocrypha include histories, historical fiction, wisdom, devotional writings, letters, and an apocalypse (a vision of the end times).

Did You Know?

The eight-day celebration of Hanukkah (the Feast of Lights in the Jewish tradition) comes from 1 Maccabees 4 and 2 Maccabees 10, when Israel reclaimed the Temple and rededicated it to God. They lit a lamp that had enough oil for only one day, but miraculously it lasted eight days.

READING THE BIBLE

Why Read the Bible?

We read the Bible for lots of different reasons. The Bible is an album of our family; it is our history. The Bible reveals who God is and who we are as creatures of God. Through the Bible we learn about God's promises to us and about how to live within the covenant relationship. We may be able to recite the commandment that Jesus gave: "Love one another as I have loved you" (John 15:12). The Bible shows us how to apply this commandment as well as the two greatest commandments: "You shall love the Lord your God with all your heart, and with all your soul, and with all your mind," and "You shall love your neighbor as yourself" (Matthew 22:37–39). It won't tell you whom to call for a date or what to study for your math test. But it will guide your important decisions. Through the Bible we come to know the very presence of God—a God who cares, guides, strengthens, comforts, and inspires us through the stories, hymns, and sayings of this amazing book.

The Bible reveals who God is and who we are as creations of God.

The Bible in Community

> *So Philip ran up to it [the chariot of an Ethiopian eunuch] and heard him reading the prophet Isaiah. He asked, "Do you understand what you are reading?" He replied, "How can I, unless someone guides me?" And he invited Philip to get in and sit beside him.*
> *(The Acts of the Apostles 8:30–31)*

This conversation between Philip and a eunuch in Acts reminds us that the Bible is meant to be read with others. The Bible is first and foremost a public book, a book that is about community and is to be heard, studied, and engaged in the company of others.

The lectionary is a list of readings from the Bible to be used throughout the year at church services.

The Episcopal Church firmly recognizes the Bible as a public book. Each Sunday we usually read four passages from the Bible—a reading from the Hebrew Scriptures, a psalm, a reading from the Epistles, and a Gospel reading. The readings are selected according to the **lectionary**, a three-year cycle of passages of the Bible read at church services. Over a three-year period, you'll hear almost all of the Christian Scriptures and a good chunk of the Hebrew Scriptures. We also hear Scriptures in our hymns and prayers found in the Book of Common Prayer. Hymn 645 ("The King of love my shepherd is"), for example, is based on Psalm 23. Our service of Holy Communion is filled with scriptural references. The Sanctus ("Holy, holy, holy") is based on Isaiah 6:3 and Revelation 4:8. Our remembrance of the Last Supper is based on 1 Corinthians 11:23–25. Through worship, we turn the hymns, letters, and stories of the Bible into prayer.

Activity: Find the lectionary in the Book of Common Prayer. On what Sunday does the lectionary begin? From what year (A, B, or C) are the readings for the current year? Many Episcopal churches follow another lectionary called the Revised Common Lectionary. Which does your church follow?

Hearing the Bible in community shows us a lot of ways to interpret it. We hear interpretations in the sermon, in the hymns, and in conversations about the sermon after worship. By reading the Bible in community we can share our insights and understandings with one another. The wisdom and insights of the community widen our understanding of the Bible, add to the richness of interpretation, and encourage us to think carefully about the biblical words we hear.

Hearing the Bible in worship also provides a particular context for how we interpret what we hear. That is, we hear the stories of the Bible in light of the good news that God loves us so much that he came to live among us as Jesus Christ. And through Christ, God gives us enduring love and forgiveness.

Steps for Reading the Bible

Don't get frustrated if you find reading the Bible isn't easy. It isn't! But there are some things you can do to make it easier. Chapter 7 discusses one method called ***lectio divina***, in which readers focus on just a few words or phrases in a Bible passage and asks God for guidance about what those words and phrases are saying to them specifically. Here are steps to read the Bible that use both your heart and your head:

1. Read the passage and ask what's important in it. Circle key words and phrases. Share these phrases with others in your study group.
2. Read the passage again, writing down any questions that come to mind. Share your questions and look together for answers.

3. Read the verses immediately before and after the passage.
4. Discuss the main themes of the passage.
5. Ask, "What is this passage calling me to do?" and share your reflections with others.

Let's go through each step.

1. *Read the passage and ask what is important in the passage. Circle key words and phrases. Share these phrases with others in your study group.*

Of course, the first step is to choose a reading. One discipline is to look at the readings for the coming Sunday or the readings in the Daily Office listed in your Book of Common Prayer. These readings begin and end in logical places such as the beginning and end of a story or parable and provide a set of readings that will help you become familiar with the diversity of experiences of God.

Read the passage. Is there anything that catches your attention? Circle key words and phrases. Share those key words and phrases with others. Reading and hearing the Bible in terms of your life today is how the Bible remains the living Word of God. While the text itself does not change, the readers do. It is likely that others in your group will be drawn to different words and phrases. We hear the stories of the Bible through our own experiences. With the guidance of the Holy Spirit, these stories become our stories.

2. *Read the passage again and write down questions that come to mind. Share your questions and look together for answers.*

While you read the passage the second time, write down questions that you have. General questions might be about how to approach the passage. Is it a hymn, a historical writing, or a code of law? Does the passage refer to unfamiliar cultural beliefs and practices? Do you recognize the characters and events in the passage?

Help one another out to find the answers. One place to look is in introductory essays and notes found in annotated bibles as well as in separate books that comment on the Bible. Introductory essays will answer general questions like these:

- What is the type of literature?
- Who wrote it?
- When was it likely written?
- What are the main themes?

A commentary will help you understand that "an eye for an eye, a tooth for a tooth" is a law that replaces more vengeful practices.

A commentary will provide further discussion of customs, ways of thinking, and symbolism of the text as well as additional word translations. Remember, the Bible wasn't first written in English. It had to be translated into English.

Context is crucial to understanding. It will help you understand, for example, that the familiar rule in Exodus, "an eye for an eye, a tooth for a tooth" (Exodus 21:23–25), carefully limited the kind of revenge that was lawful—at a time when other societies were allowed to put people to death for minor crimes.

As you continue your study of the Bible, you'll improve your skills for answering questions and grow in knowledge of the world in which the Bible was written. Don't worry if you can't find answers to all your questions. But continue to keep them in mind as you explore the meaning of the passage.

3. *Read the verses just prior to and after the passage.*

The verses just before and after the passage often provide great insight into the meaning of your reading. For example, the story of the woman who poured expensive oil over Jesus' head in Matthew 26 comes just before the Last Supper. Knowing this context shows us that her action wasn't a random act of adoration; pouring oil on Jesus was preparing his body for death and, for readers, foreshadows the crucifixion.

4. *Discuss the main themes of the passage.*

Once you have a sense of the context, look back at the words and phrases you circled. These will help you identify the main themes of the passage. Discuss these themes with people in your group. Ask each other if these themes remind you of other stories in the Bible. If so, which ones? See if these themes remind you of experiences in your own life. Do these other stories help you understand the passage? If you were reading the eye-for-an-eye passage in Exodus, you might remember that Jesus taught a new standard of mercy and forgiveness: to love your enemies, do good to those who hate you, and to turn the other cheek (Luke 6:29 and Matthew 5:39).

Activity: Beginning on page 867, the Book of Common Prayer reprints the Articles of Religion adopted in 1801. According to Article VI, what "containeth all things necessary for salvation"?

5. *Ask, "What is this passage calling me to do?" and share your reflections with others.*

The final step is to apply the themes and messages to your thoughts and beliefs of today. The Bible is the living Word of God meant to help us understand God, ourselves, and our world. Ask one another, "How does this passage challenge your thoughts and beliefs?" Again, be aware of the original context of the writing. The Bible was written by people living in a specific time and culture that was probably quite different from yours. Consider your answer in terms of the practices and teachings of your faith community. Your faith community can be particularly helpful with this final step. A community will give you a variety of viewpoints and a wealth of knowledge and experience that will help you explore the meaning of the passage in your life.

There is no substitute for setting aside time to read and study regularly. It's the only way to develop an understanding of the Bible.

READ THE BIBLE: IT'S YOUR FAMILY ALBUM

The Bible reflects our central beliefs: The Lord is our God, the Lord alone; God freed us from our life of sin by sending his only Son to die on the cross and raising him from the dead. Read the Bible as a family album that tells you who God is, who you are, and what all of us together are called to do as people of God. The struggles of the people you read about in the Bible are often a lot like our own struggles today. The life, ministry, and teachings of Jesus will help guide us in our lives today. His death and resurrection give us new life today.

Chapter 3

Knowing Our History

Our history tells us who we are. When we make new friends, we often share stories about ourselves. We share with each other where we were born, significant events in our lives such as when we learned to ride a bicycle, the cities where we've lived, and places we've visited.

This is my history: As you learned in the last chapter, I was born in Pine Bluff, Arkansas. A few years later, we moved to Highland, New York, where my parents still live today. We chose to attend Christ Episcopal Church in Poughkeepsie and five years later, when I was nine years old, I was baptized. I chose to be baptized. The whole congregation gathered to share in my baptism. The children in Sunday school processed into the service with the verger, acolytes, choir, and priest, and each poured a little bit of water into the font. Everyone gathered around the font to see the priest pouring water over my head and promised to help me grow in faith.

That was many, many years ago now. But it is part of who I am and forms the choices I make today. I believe God calls each of us to be his child and calls the entire community to support each person in his or her life in Christ. The beliefs I have today are formed by my experience at baptism.

Parents and Mentors

The book *Lesser Feasts and Fasts* includes short biographies of people in our church history along with appointed prayers and readings for each saint's day. Look on page 19 of the Book of Common Prayer through the list of saints and identify any names you recognize. What do you know about them?

You have your own unique stories that tell who you are, too. History isn't just something that happened in the past. We carry our histories with us in our thoughts and in our actions. It's part of who we are.

Each of our personal histories began when we were a mass of cells in our mother's womb, surrounded by a cushion of water as each of our parts was formed in beautiful detail. Psalm 139 reminds us that God was at our beginning, knitting us each individually into the person we were meant to be.

For you yourself created my inmost parts;
you knit me together in my mother's womb.
I will thank you, for I am marvelously made;
Your works are wonderful, and I know it well. (Psalm 139:12–13)

GOD IS AT OUR BEGINNING

Our history also includes the stories of God's family that we read in the Bible. God swept over the face of the waters and called all creation into being from nothing. God created humankind. God called Abraham out of the city of Ur and onto a journey with the promise of as many descendents as there are stars—he became the father of the Israelites. God delivered the Israelites from the death of slavery in Egypt to new life in their Promised Land of Canaan. This is our history, too. Just as God remained with the Israelites through forty years of wandering in the wilderness and gave them everything they needed, God remains with us today and gives us what we need.

Our history is also with Jesus, God's Son, who lived among us proclaiming the coming of the kingdom of God, teaching how to live a life of love, and healing the sick and the lame. Our history is with the disciples of Jesus who shared in Jesus' life and ministry, who witnessed his death, and who spread the good news of his resurrection. Being an Episcopalian is all this history, and more.

HISTORY OF THE CHURCH

To be an Episcopalian is only one way of being a Christian. In fact, there are more than 340 kinds of Christian churches in the world today. The Episcopal Church is a particularly American church that was established in the late 1700s. It's part of the **Anglican Communion** that includes the Church of England and thirty-seven other churches around the world. The Episcopal Church grew out of the Church of England, which broke off from the Roman Catholic Church in the sixteenth century. But our history is much more than a list of dates, and it's much older than four hundred years.

The Birth of the Church

> *So those who welcomed his message were baptized, and that day about three thousand persons were added. They devoted themselves to the apostles' teaching and fellowship, to the breaking of bread and the prayers.* (Acts 2:41–42)

Fifty days after the resurrection of Jesus, on the day of **Pentecost**, the Holy Spirit came down from heaven like a violent wind. The apostles' tongues were on fire and they began to speak in other languages. Filled with the Holy Spirit, the apostles began to follow the **Great Commission** that Jesus had given them:

> *Go therefore and make disciples of all nations, baptizing them in the name of the Father and of the Son and of the Holy Spirit, and teaching them to obey everything that I have commanded you. And remember, I am with you always, to the end of the age.* (Matthew 28:19–20)

As Christians we understand ourselves as being called to this same Great Commission in our lives.

On that day of Pentecost, the apostles baptized those who believed and the church began. The word "church" in this sense does not refer to a building, but to a community of believers. Today we often call Pentecost "the birthday of the church."

After Jesus' resurrection, the apostles spread the teachings of Jesus in Jewish communities near Jerusalem and outside Jerusalem during mission journeys. These early communities considered themselves to be Jews who followed Jesus and to be a reform movement within Judaism, or the Jewish religion. It wasn't until about 90 C.E., nearly 60 years after Jesus' death and resurrection, that the followers of Christ began to be called "Christians."

The Apostle Paul played a big part in spreading Christianity. He started out persecuting Christians but on the road to the city of Damascus, in what is now the country of Syria, a few years after Jesus died everything changed. Paul met Jesus for the first time through a vision telling him to spread the good news to the Gentiles, that is, people who were not descendants of the Israelites. Paul and his partners began to establish Christian communities throughout the area around the Mediterranean Sea, which was at that time controlled by the Romans and was part of the Roman Empire. These early communities, who believed that the world as they knew it would end soon when Jesus returned, attended the Jewish Temple daily and shared meals, teachings, and prayers in one another's homes. New converts joined the community through baptism and they broke bread to remember Christ's death and resurrection. Baptism and the breaking of the bread are the two central sacraments of the church today.

During this time, the Roman Empire extended as far west as Spain and Great Britain and as far east as the Persian Gulf; as far north as Germany and as far south as northern Africa.

Communities of the Early Church

The map on page 18 of Chapter 2 shows the location of many early church communities. Antioch, Ephesus, Alexandria, Corinth, and Rome, the larger cities of the Roman Empire connected by trading routes, had big Christian communities. During the first few hundred years after Jesus' resurrection, the rest of the world had no—or at least very little—knowledge of Jesus. Christianity began as small communities in a specific region of the world—the Roman Empire—and from there it spread from Asia into Europe and Africa. And during the sixteenth century, colonization spread Christianity to the Americas. Today Christian churches exist throughout the world.

Activity: Find the Mediterranean Sea on a modern map. What modern countries were once part of the Roman Empire in the first century?

Episkopos *in the Early Church*

The apostles were the leaders of the early church and had the authority of Jesus' teaching. The leader of local Christian communities was called *episkopos*, or "overseer." The word "Episcopal" in fact comes from the Greek word *episkopos*, and the English word for *episkopos* is "bishop." In the Episcopal Church, the bishop oversees the diocese, the primary geographic and administrative unit of the Episcopal Church. Early Christians also referred to their local leader as *presbyteros* (presbyter or priest) and *diakonos* (deacon). Today the Episcopal Church has a threefold ordained ministry of bishop, priest, and deacon, each with a different role in the church. The apostles passed their authority to local leaders by laying their hands on the new leaders. So, as the apostles died, new leaders were chosen and the authority of the apostles' teaching was continued. This is called **apostolic succession**. Apostolic succession and a threefold ministry

A bishop is the chief priest and pastor of a diocese.

of bishops, priests, and deacons are defining characteristics of the Episcopal Church.

The Roman Empire to the Middle Ages

In 324 C.E., Constantine became the first Roman emperor to convert to Christianity. Until that time, Christians were at times persecuted by fines, imprisonment, and even death for refusing to worship Roman gods. When Constantine gained control over the entire Roman Empire, he moved its capital from Rome to Byzantium in what is now the city of Istanbul, Turkey. He renamed the city "Nova Roma," or New Rome, but it was popularly known as Constantinople (the city of Constantine). Constantinople later became the center of Eastern Orthodox Christianity, while Rome became the center of Western catholic Christianity. Constantine saw Christianity as a way to unify his vast empire and began the process of creating a uniform belief by calling the bishops together in 325 C.E. to Nicea, located in the present-day city of Iznik, Turkey. Their job was to find a common understanding of Jesus and his place in history. The result was the Nicene Creed that we recite at church every Sunday.

Activity: The Apostles' Creed dates from the fourth century. Find the Apostles' Creed and the Nicene Creed in the Book of Common Prayer. During what liturgies is the Apostles' Creed said? The Nicene Creed? Which of the two is a personal statement of faith?

By the fifth century, the Roman Empire had grown weak from invasion by tribes from northern Europe and political fighting in Rome. The end of Roman rule began the eleven-hundred-year period from about 400 to 1500 C.E. that we call the **Middle Ages**. The western empire (Europe) broke into small regions with several languages, each ruled by different kings and noblemen. The church provided both religious and cultural unity for Europe. The Roman emperor still ruled the eastern part of the Roman Empire until 1071, when Muslim Turkish rulers from Asia conquered the city of Byzantium.

> Muslims believe in the same God as the Jews and Christians. The Muslim religion, called Islam, was begun in 610 C.E. by the prophet Mohammed.

During the Middle Ages, communities were organized around land owned by local noblemen and protected by knights. The peasants worked the land and produced goods for the nobility in exchange for protection. The church, particularly monasteries, owned much of the land and became increasingly involved in social, political, and business aspects of daily life. Many monasteries were responsible for the spiritual as well as the economic and physical well-being of the people. Monks and nuns prepared medicine, sewed, and taught reading and writing. Monasteries were also the libraries of society and preserved important early Christian writings. We see how important the church was to life in the Middle Ages by the magnificent cathedrals the church built in city and town centers such as the cathedrals of Nôtre Dame in Chartes and in Paris, France.

The Middle Ages were also the time of the Crusades. You may have seen movies such as *Kingdom of Heaven*, or learned about the Crusades in history class. The Crusades, which lasted about a hundred years, were launched in 1095 by the church to recover the Holy Land—the region of the world where the stories of the Bible took place and where Jesus lived—from the Muslims. The kings and other leaders in Europe supported the Crusades to acquire land, riches, and control over trading routes. During the Crusades all non-Christians, especially Jews and Muslims, were targets of persecution.

THE REFORMATION

As the Roman Catholic Church grew more wealthy and powerful, church leaders limited the people's freedom to express opposing ideas. The church used its power over the spiritual lives of the people to sell indulgences—pieces of paper that guaranteed entry into heaven. Some people believed indulgences were abuses of church power and violated the teachings of the Bible.

Martin Luther (1483–1546) was a leader of the Reformation in Germany.

People began to protest these and other practices and called for reforms. This movement, which gained in strength in the sixteenth century, is called the **Reformation**. **Martin Luther** of Germany and **John Calvin** of France were two leaders of the Reformation in Europe.

Martin Luther's most famous act was nailing ninety-five theses—

or arguments—on the door of the castle church in Wittenberg in 1517. The theses stated his disagreements with the Roman Catholic Church, including the selling of indulgences. He argued against the Roman Catholic teaching that salvation came through the church. Instead, Luther promoted a doctrine, or belief, called **justification by grace through faith**. This doctrine states that God gives people salvation freely. We cannot earn salvation with good deeds, but we can accept it with faith. Luther believed that people didn't need the church between them and God, and that sacraments weren't necessary for salvation.

Justification by grace through faith is the teaching that we accept God's free gift of salvation by believing in God.

Meanwhile, in France, John Calvin accepted Luther's doctrine of justification by grace through faith. But he also believed in the fundamental doctrine of predestination. Predestination is the belief that God directs the course of history down to the smallest detail. It's the job of people to maintain the order created by God.

The Reformation resulted in the establishment of Protestant churches that broke with the traditional practices of the Roman Catholic Church. Both Luther and Calvin were important to this movement.

In earlier centuries, some people had opposed doctrines of the Roman Catholic Church. So what made the Protestant Reformation take off in the fifteenth century? Historians agree that the printing press played a big part in the Reformation's success. The printing press, first used in Europe in the mid-1400s, allowed differing opinions to be widely distributed, strengthening the Reformation movement.

The Reformation and the printing press also helped make it possible to produce early translations of the Bible from Latin, the official language of the church, to the languages people spoke every day, such as French or German or English. New ways of believing encouraged people to come to their own decisions about faith, so they needed to read the Bible in their own languages. By 1524, Luther had translated the New Testament into German, and by 1526, **William Tyndale** had translated it into English. This brought the words of the Bible and its interpretation into the hands of believers, not just educated priests and monks.

John Wycliff first translated the Bible into English in the late 1300s, but because it was written before the introduction of the printing press in Europe, it was written by hand and was not as widely read as the Tyndale translation.

England during the Reformation

The Episcopal Church traces its roots directly to the Church of England, which, until King **Henry VIII**, was part of the Roman Catholic Church. So to understand our history, we need to know what was going on in England during this time.

The Church of England had always recognized the pope in Rome as the head of the church, and when the Reformation first began, Henry the VIII supported the pope. For his loyal support, the pope named Henry VIII the "Defender of the Faith." Soon after, though, a disagreement broke out. Henry VIII asked the pope to annul, or end, his marriage with Catherine of Aragon because she did not give Henry a son to inherit the throne. The pope refused to grant Henry an annulment, so in 1534, King Henry issued an "Act of Supremacy" that made him head of the Church of England, splitting the Church of England from the Roman Catholic Church.

Because the Church of England did not split over differences of belief, unlike the Protestant churches, the Church of England kept many of the practices and beliefs of the Roman Catholic Church, including its system of government by bishops and its style of worship. Like Protestant churches, the Church of England worshipped in the language of the people, in this case English, and the Church of England affirmed that salvation comes from God's grace, not from the deeds of the believer.

Activity: In the Book of Common Prayer you can find historical documents of the church. Find the preface for the first Book of Common Prayer. When was the first Book of Common Prayer written? In what language did the prayer book require all things to be read and sung in the church?

The Anglican Church in North America

Earlier we said that the Episcopal Church is uniquely American. And that's true. Our history has greatly affected who we are, how we worship together, and how we govern ourselves. And it will continue to help define us into the future.

Just as Americans began to see themselves as a new nation apart from England and the crown, members of the Church of England in America also saw their church as separate from the Church of England. In 1607, the settlement of Jamestown, Virginia, organized itself as a parish with a priest brought from England and supported its clergy with local government taxes. Because these settlers provided for their own

> In the 1600s a parish was a geographic area of land that financially supported its own church with taxes

financial needs, they began to see themselves as independent of the Church of England. The situation was a little different in the northern colonies because taxes in northern New England supported the Congregational Church, not the Anglican Church. In New England, Anglicans kept closer ties to England because religious societies in England paid for their priests.

During the colonial period, no bishops ever visited America. The leaders of the Church of England and the British Parliament didn't want to grant American communities the independence that having a bishop would provide. But the colonists didn't really mind—as long as they had a sufficient number of priests, they were happy to be far from the rule of the Church of England.

A group of bishops in both Scotland and England did not require bishops to swear allegiance to the crown. These nonjuring bishops had refused to break their allegiance to King James II, who was deposed in 1688.

American Bishops

After the Revolution, the New England Anglicans wanted to organize themselves formally and felt they needed a bishop. In June 1783, they sent **Samuel Seabury**, the rector of a church in the state of New York, to England to be consecrated, or to be made, a bishop. Because Samuel Seabury was an American citizen and couldn't take the Oath of the King's Supremacy, the English bishops couldn't consecrate him a bishop. Seabury turned to the bishops in Scotland, who weren't under English law. In November 1784, they consecrated Samuel Seabury as the first American bishop.

Samuel Seabury was the Episcopal Church's first American bishop. (National Portrait Gallery, Smithsonian Institution)

Two years later, the British Parliament granted the Archbishop of Canterbury the right to consecrate three American bishops who wouldn't be asked to swear allegiance to the crown. By 1790, three American bishops had been consecrated by bishops in England, enough to bring the historic episcopate, or system of governance by bishops, to America.

Birth of the Episcopal Church

When Samuel Seabury returned to America, he tried to unify the various Anglican churches as one American Episcopal Church. It wasn't an easy job. The communities in the North wanted to have bishops, while those in the South had gotten used to governing themselves without a bishop. The two groups compromised: They would have bishops, but the priests and members of the congregations would help choose bishops and write church canons, or laws.

In 1789, the leaders of the new Episcopal Church wrote a constitution. It said that bishops would be elected by the priests and the members of congregations instead of being appointed by the king or queen, as was done in England. The Episcopal Church would be governed by two houses—the House of Bishops, comprised only of bishops, and the House of Deputies, comprised of clergy, or priests, and general church members. Laws can originate in either house but both houses must agree on them. The two-house system was much like the two-house system of the U.S. Congress.

The year 1789 was a banner year for the Episcopal Church. It held its first General Convention, passed its constitution, and adopted the first American **Book of Common Prayer**. The American Book of Common Prayer was much the same as the prayer book in England, minus prayers for the king and royal family. Plus, it added a call to the Holy Spirit, or **epiclesis**, in the Eucharistic prayer, a promise Samuel Seabury had made to the Scottish bishops when he was consecrated.

The first Book of Common Prayer provided liturgies, prayers, and instructions so that all members of the church could share in common worship. It was first written in England in 1549 and adopted by the Act of Uniformity.

Activity: Look at Eucharistic Prayer A in your Book of Common Prayer. Can you find the epiclesis? (Look particularly on page 363.) Write it below.

The Episcopal Church in the 1800s

The Episcopal Church continued to be shaped by the life and culture of the United States. During the 1800s, the West was settled, the Civil War was fought, American industry expanded, and a great number of people from Ireland, Germany, Scandinavia, southern Europe, and Asia immigrated to the United States. Immigration changed the country from a nation of people with largely British backgrounds to a diverse people with a variety of practices and beliefs. Worship practices and social activity became likewise more diverse in the Episcopal Church.

Westward Expansion and Missionaries

During its first few decades, the Episcopal Church struggled. General Conventions were poorly attended, several dioceses had no bishops, and membership didn't grow. But along came **John Henry Hobart**, with his great energy and enthusiasm for evangelism. As Bishop of New York from 1816 to 1830, he was responsible for establishing Episcopal churches in nearly every major town in New York State, increasing their number from 50 to 170. During his first four years as bishop, the number of clergy doubled and the number of missionaries quadrupled. By 1820, the number of Episcopal churches in the United States had doubled to 400.

In 1835, the General Convention consecrated missionary bishops who, instead of overseeing an established diocese, were sent to the frontier to establish new dioceses. **Jackson Kemper** was the first missionary bishop. Traveling by horseback and open wagon, he organized eight dioceses and established two colleges. Kemper worked among Potowatami, Seneca, Oneida, and Huron Indians, urged the church to pay more attention to Native Americans, and encouraged the translation of the Bible and prayer book into their native languages.

Jackson Kemper's unofficial title was "The Bishop of the Whole Northwest."

Jackson Kemper ordained **Enmegahbowh**, an Odawa (Ottawa) Indian from Canada, as a deacon in 1859. Twelve years later in 1867, Enmegahbowh became the first recognized Native American priest in the Episcopal Church. In 1869, Paul Mazakute was ordained the first Dakota priest, and in 1881, **David Pendleton Oakerhater** became the first Cheyenne deacon. These men worked hard, often without the support of the national church, to spread the gospel among Native American people.

The church's hard work in the missions paid off. From 1820 to 1859, the number of Episcopal congregations grew from 400 to 2,120.

African Americans and the Civil War

America was a place of slavery and racial bigotry. Just after the Revolutionary War, 800,000 African Americans were slaves; only 59,000 lived as free citizens. America was also a place of great change. **Absalom Jones**, born into slavery in 1746, purchased his wife's and his own freedom and later became the first African American to be ordained a priest in the Episcopal Church.

Jones and other blacks had left St. George's Methodist Church in Philadelphia when ushers told them that all African Americans had to sit apart from the whites in the balcony. He and others walked out and began another church that later joined the Episcopal family, as St. Thomas African Episcopal Church. Before the Civil War began, fifteen other African Americans were ordained Episcopal priests.

Activity: "The Calendar of the Church Year" in the Book of Common Prayer lists the lesser feasts and fasts of the church. When is Absalom Jones's feast day?

Just as the nation was divided about slavery across North-South lines, so was the Episcopal Church. Southern agriculture depended on slave labor, so Southerners supported slavery. Southern Episcopal plantation owners built churches for their black slaves, who were ministered to by white clergy. Northerners, for the most part, wanted to do away with slavery, but some northern white churches divided their members according to the color of their skin. The Episcopal Church never took an official position on slavery.

Absalom Jones is the first African-American priest. He was ordained in 1802. (Raphaelle Peale, *Absalom Jones*, 1810, oil on paper mounted to board, Delaware Art Museum. Gift of Absalom Jones School, 1971. Reproduced with permission.)

When the South seceded from the United States and declared itself a separate nation, many southern dioceses organized themselves as a breakaway church called the Protestant Episcopal Church in the Confederate States of America. The northern church didn't recognize the split and continued to list southern bishops on the roster at general conventions. At the end of the Civil War, the southern dioceses were invited to return to the Episcopal Church; in 1865, the Episcopal Church was once again united.

Rise of Industry and the Church's Response to Social Problems

After the end of the Civil War, American industry grew by leaps and bounds, moving from fourth place to first in the entire world. As people moved away from farms and small towns to seek jobs—and opportunity—

in the factories, and newcomers came to America from other countries, our cities grew quickly. But the factories offered poor working conditions, low wages, and long hours. Many employed children. Two new groups of people, or social classes, came into existence—the working poor and the wealthy capitalists (those with money to build the factories and make money from them). New social problems appeared, too—unemployment, unsafe working conditions, child labor, and poor housing.

The Industrial Revolution created a large poor working class in our nation's cities and a smaller class of wealthy capitalists.

Episcopalians, who believe strongly in helping people in need, responded with action. Trinity Church Wall Street, in New York City, a wealthy parish that owned a lot of land there, fixed the apartments they owned to help improve housing conditions. The Women's Auxiliary, organized in 1871, provided most of the money for churchwide programs to help the poor. In 1883, **William Rainsford**, rector at St. George's in New York City, created clubs for girls, boys, women, and men, as well as societies for lots of different interest groups. He also built church schools with gyms for the city's poor children, and started parish nursing programs.

Activity: Find the "Articles of Religion" in the Book of Common Prayer. What does the church say of good works?

Earlier in the 1800s, many churches were unfriendly places for people who were poor and uneducated. It was not uncommon for churches to raise funds by charging parishioners rent to sit in a pew—or bench—on Sunday morning. William Augustus Muhlenberg, founder of the Church of the Holy Communion in New York City, did away with the pew tax. He also started a parish school, a parish unemployment fund, and a fresh-air fund to send poor city children into the country for the summer. Muhlenberg also introduced his church to some traditionally Roman Catholic practices, such as weekly communion, altar flowers, choir robes, Christmas decorations, and special services for Holy Week, the days when Christians recall Jesus' crucifixion and death. But Muhlenberg still held on to the Protestant emphasis on a personal experience with God.

The Oxford Movement

Muhlenberg's introduction of "Catholic" traditions paved the way for other "high-church" practices in other parishes around the country. Followers of the **Oxford Movement**, started in England in 1833, wanted the

Episcopal Church to re-adopt Roman Catholic practices such as putting candles on the altar, having priests wear chasubles and other vestments, carrying a big cross down the aisle at the beginning of Sunday services, and bowing. With huge numbers of immigrants from Roman Catholic backgrounds arriving in America during these years, many newcomers to the Episcopal Church felt at home with these rituals.

A chasuble is the sleeveless poncho-like vestment worn by the celebrant at Eucharist.

Many other people, however, were offended by these rituals and felt they were too similar to Roman Catholic practices. They worried that these formal rituals would make the Episcopal Church similar to the Roman Catholic Church in other ways, too. They feared that a more "Roman" Episcopal Church would try to exert power over people's individual beliefs.

This controversy, also known as the "ritualist controversy," was a very big deal. For example, the Bishop of the Diocese of Massachusetts refused to visit a Boston church because it had candles and a crucifix on the altar and its rector wore vestments. In 1868, the General Convention considered a proposal to ban such practices. But Presiding Bishop John Henry Hopkins felt that diversity was good for the church and kept most of these practices in place. Only bowing and lifting the bread and the wine during the Eucharist as acts of adoration were forbidden.

Activity: What are the worship practices at your church? Are candles placed on the altar? Who is in the procession? Does your church have a stone altar? Is the altar highly decorated or plain? How does this affect your worship experience?

The Episcopal Church in the 1900s and Early 2000s

The 1900s were marked by concerns for worldwide church unity, continuing social issues, and the role of women in the church.

Church Unity

In the late 1800s and early 1900s, American church leaders wondered whether the various American church denominations (Baptists, Methodists, Lutherans, Roman Catholics) could address modern problems more effectively as one body. William Reed Huntington, an Episcopal priest, outlined four principles that the Episcopal Church believes are necessary to restore all denominations as one church. This important document for the Episcopal Church became known as the Chicago Quadrilateral and appears in the Book of Common Prayer in the section called "Historical Documents." In the early 1900s, **Charles Henry Brent**, an Episcopal bishop, led the way toward worldwide church unity. In 1927, he presided over the World Conference on Faith and Order, which later became part of the **World Council of Churches**, an organization of more than 340 Christian denominations worldwide.

This is the symbol for the World Council of Churches. Its website is oikoumene.org.

The Episcopal Church still works toward unity with other churches. In 1950, the Episcopal Church helped found the National Council of Churches (nccusa.org). In 2000, the Episcopal Church and the Evangelical Lutheran Church of America established full communion (a union) with one another. The two churches fully recognize each other's members, ministries, and sacraments, and can share one another's priests and pastors. Formal discussions of communion continue between the Episcopal Church and the Moravian and Presbyterian Churches.

African Americans and the Episcopal Church

The Episcopal Church will always be engaged in social issues. Just as the United States was largely segregated after World War II, so was the Episcopal Church, and segregation and racism were big issues in the church in the 1950s and '60s. While the Episcopal Church had black bishops, their congregations were likely to be black, too. African Americans had been attending seminaries since the 1800s and in the 1950s, the Episcopal Church began to welcome both African Americans and whites at the same seminaries. But during that decade, many of the mostly white Episcopal congregations in inner cities left the cities for the suburbs.

In the 1960s, the Episcopal Church began to work more actively to end racism, by supporting Civil Rights laws and giving time and money to organizations that worked to end social inequalities. Each August 14 we remember **Jonathan Daniels**, a young European-American Episcopalian martyred in the Civil Rights movement. Some dioceses merged black and white congregations and, in 1969, **John Burgess** was elected the first African-American diocesan bishop to serve an American diocese. Today about 3 percent of Episcopal priests and 8 percent of bishops are African American. The Episcopal Church continues to struggle against racism to this day.

The Episcopal Church among Native Americans

The history of the Episcopal Church among Native Americans isn't a proud one. The 1606 charter of Jamestown, Virginia, called for the Church of England to convert the "infidels and savages" who "live in darkness and miserable ignorance of true knowledge." In the late 1800s, the Episcopal Church established missions among Indians of the Southwest but rarely supported these ministries financially or permitted Native Americans to be ordained to the priesthood.

In the latter half of the twentieth century, the church began to work harder to respect the spirituality of Native Americans and welcome them to full participation in the church. Two Native Americans—David Pendleton Oakerhater and Enmegahbowh—are celebrated for their ministry with native Americans. In 1977 the General Convention created Navajoland Area Mission from parts of the Dioceses of Arizona, Utah, and Rio Grande in New Mexico as a diocese of its own, serving the Navajo Nation. The General Convention of 1997 designated a Decade of Remembrance, Recognition, and Reconciliation "for welcoming Native Peoples into congregational life and developing an outreach partnership among urban Native Peoples." The church also has a Native American Ministries Office at its churchwide headquarters in New York City.

Role of Women

In 1889 the Episcopal Church began the office of female deaconate as a way for young single women to help care for the needs of the poor and sick and to train young people in the faith. But deaconesses didn't have a liturgy of ordination in the Book of Common Prayer, and had to resign if they married.

The Episcopal Church also revived religious orders for women. In 1845, **Anne Ayres**, a parishioner of the Church of the Holy Communion in New York City, became the first American religious sister in the Anglican tradition. But women still weren't invited to leadership positions in the church.

From the 1920s to the 1950s, the number of deaconesses declined. Instead, many women interested in serving the church worked as directors of Christian education or teachers at seminaries.

It wasn't until the 1960s and 1970s that women gained equal rights within the church. Deaconesses gained the right to marry in 1964, and in

Did You Know?

In 1944, Florence Li Tim-Oi became the first woman ordained a priest in the Anglican Communion. She was ordained in Hong Kong to minister to Chinese refugees in Japanese-occupied China.

1970, women were allowed to serve as lay readers and deputies to General Convention. After a resolution in 1973 to open the priesthood to women, eleven women deacons—known as the "Philadelphia eleven"—were ordained on July 29, 1974 by three retired bishops.

The Rt. Rev. Barbara Harris was the first woman bishop in the Episcopal Church of the United States. (photo credit: Robert Burgess)

Two years later, the General Convention changed canon law to allow women into the threefold ministry of bishop, priest, and deacon. In 1989, **Barbara Clementine Harris** became the first woman consecrated a bishop in the Episcopal Church. Although women may be ordained deacons and priests, it's up to each diocese whether to do so. Today three dioceses in the United States still refuse to ordain or recognize the priesthood of women (Fort Worth in Texas; Quincy in Illinois; and San Joaquin in California).

In 2003 the General Convention approved the consecration of **V. Gene Robinson**, an openly gay priest, as bishop of New Hampshire. This action has threatened to divide the Episcopal Church internally and from the worldwide Anglican Communion.

Ministry of Youth

In the Episcopal Church today, the ministry of youth gets lots of attention. In 1982, the Episcopal Church held its first Episcopal Youth Event, a gathering of over a thousand youth from throughout the Episcopal Church, including Latin American and Caribbean dioceses, and international participants. Every three years, young people from across the country and around the world gather for a week of worship, fellowship, and learning. Young people themselves design and plan the services, and lead music and worship. Each of the Episcopal Church's nine provinces also sends two youth to participate in the Official Youth Presence at the General Convention. As members of your faith community, you're important to the ministry of your parish. This book can help you explore all the ways you can get involved in your parish and your world.

THE EPISCOPAL CHURCH TODAY

The Episcopal Church today has over seven thousand parishes and missions and 2.3 million active baptized members, about 800,000 of whom regularly attend Sunday worship. Fifty-eight percent of Episcopal laypeople and 27 percent of clergy are women.

The Episcopal Church still works hard for greater unity among all churches, and takes social issues just as seriously as ever. The Episcopal Church maintains an Office of Government Relations in Washington, D.C., to advocate for the poor, the environment, and other social issues in U.S. government. Internationally, the Episcopal Church cooperates with Anglican churches worldwide to provide relief to those in Africa suffering with HIV/AIDS. All young men in the United States must register with the Selective Service within thirty days of their eighteenth birthday. While the Episcopal Church is committed, with all churches in the Anglican Communion, to achieving peace and justice through nonviolent means and opposes the aggressive use of war, the views about participation in the armed forces vary greatly with the church. The Episcopal Church acknowledges that prayerful consideration leads some members to choose to participate in the armed forces (conscientious participation) and others to object to participating in or preparing for war (conscientious objection). The Offices of the Ministries with Young People publishes balanced and faith-based information to help you discern your views about this issue. These are only a few examples of the many ways in which the Episcopal Church continues to work for justice and peace in the world, both at home and abroad.

The Episcopal Church, with roots in the Church of England and George Washington as one of its early members, has traditionally been a church that welcomed diversity. About 5 percent of Episcopalians are black and 2 percent Latino. About seventy-two Episcopal Churches have predominantly Asian congregations. Our people, our buildings, and our styles of worship vary greatly, but we are a people bound by a shared faith, common mission, and common worship.

Chapter 4

Faith: What Do We Believe?

Jesus said to him, "Go; your faith has made you well." Immediately he regained his sight and followed him on the way. (Mark 10:52)

In a few words, *"Go; your faith has made you well,"* Jesus healed blind Bartimaeus. Without sight, the world was threatening, dangerous, and very small. Blind Bartimaeus made a life begging at the side of the road, taking more than giving. But sensing that Jesus was near, Bartimaeus cried out, "Have mercy." Jesus answered, "What do you want me to do for you?" Bartimaeus might have wanted anything—food or shelter or enough money to take care of all his needs. But he asked for sight. "My teacher, let me see again." Jesus responded, "Go; your faith has made you well."

Bartimaeus' faith gave him a new *way of seeing*, and it showed him a world filled with light, hope, and possibility. He was so changed by this new way of seeing that he got up immediately and followed Jesus. Just like that, he became a disciple.

Our faith is a new way of seeing, too. Expressing our belief in God changes how we see the world. Instead of an indifferent planet, our world is a place in which God blesses us and invites us to respond with loving actions. When we see the world as God wants us to see it, we're invited to become disciples of Jesus, just like Bartimaeus. But what exactly is it that our faith leads us to believe?

STATEMENTS OF FAITH

We have three statements of faith in the Episcopal Church—the Nicene Creed, the Apostles' Creed, and the Athanasian Creed. We say the Nicene Creed during the Holy Eucharist and the Apostles' Creed during the Service of Baptism and when we say the "Daily Office" of Morning Prayer and Evening Prayer in the Book of Common Prayer. You can find the Athanasian Creed among the historical documents in the Book of Common Prayer.

Episcopalians say the Nicene Creed as part of Holy Eucharist, and the Apostles' Creed at baptisms, Morning Prayer, and Evening Prayer.

Activity: The Athanasian Creed is printed on page 864 in the "Historical Documents" section of the Book of Common Prayer. What is its Latin name?

These creeds are ancient statements of belief that grew out of questions and disputes in the early years of the church. Who exactly are Jesus and the Holy Spirit? Is the Holy Spirit also divine? Is Jesus both divine and human? If we believe in God the Father, the Son, and the Holy Spirit, do we still believe in one God? How are the Father, the Son, and the Holy Spirit related? Church councils in Nicea and Chalcedon, towns in present-day Turkey, met during the fourth and fifth centuries to ponder these questions, and in response wrote the Nicene Creed. The Nicene Creed begins with the word "We" because it is a statement of faith by a community.

The **Apostles' Creed** developed from the answers to the questions the church asked candidates for baptism in the early years of Christianity. Those questions are:

> Do you believe in God the Father?
> Do you believe in Jesus Christ, the Son of God?
> Do you believe in God the Holy Spirit?

Candidates for baptism—or their godparents—continue to answer these very same questions today. The Apostles' Creed is a personal statement of belief, so it begins with the word "I"—"I believe in God, the Father, almighty."

The Apostles' Creed

Before we look closely at the Apostles' Creed, take a minute or two to read it slowly. Notice that it has three parts.

I believe in God, the Father almighty,
creator of heaven and earth.

I believe in Jesus Christ, his only Son, our Lord.
He was conceived by the power of the Holy Spirit
and born of the Virgin Mary.
He suffered under Pontius Pilate,
was crucified, died, and was buried.
He descended to the dead.
On the third day he rose again.
He ascended into heaven,
and is seated at the right hand of the Father.
He will come again to judge the living and the dead.

I believe in the Holy Spirit,
the holy catholic Church,
the communion of saints,
the forgiveness of sins,
the resurrection of the body,
and the life everlasting.

Belief

The Apostles' Creed begins with the words "I believe *in* God." It doesn't say, "*I believe that there is a* God." That's an important difference. We're not asserting that God exists—God exists whether we believe or not. We're saying we have a relationship with God. The word creed comes from the Latin word *credere*, meaning "what I put my heart (or my trust) in." So when we proclaim our belief in God, what we're really saying is, "I give my heart to God." What a difference this makes! By giving our hearts to God, we're entering into a relationship of trust. The creeds are statements about the God we love and trust.

Substituting the words "I love" for the words "I believe" in the Apostles' Creed changes the creed from a statement about existence into a statement about relationship.

The Trinity

The Apostles' Creed (like the Nicene Creed) has three parts because we believe in One God in three persons: Father, Son, and Holy Spirit. Our belief in one God who exists in three eternal, distinct, and equal persons is called the **Trinity**. The word "trinity" comes from two Latin words—*tri* meaning three and *unitas* meaning unity. God's nature is three persons united in one God.

Activity: The first lines of each of the three sections of the Nicene Creed also express the Trinity. Find the Nicene Creed in your Book of Common Prayer. What does each sentence say about how the three persons are related to one another as One God?

There's more to our understanding of the Trinity. We believe that the three persons that are One God are *one*, *equal*, and *coeternal*.

One. Try thinking about the Trinity as similar to the parts of time: Time is composed of past, present, and the future. Each is distinct from the other, yet each is an expression of the same concept, that is, time. The past doesn't represent one kind of time, the present another, and the future still another. They are *one*. Likewise, God the Father, God the Son, and God the Holy Spirit are each distinct persons, yet each is God.

Parents and Mentors

Which of the three persons—the Father, the Son, or the Holy Spirit—do you most often address your prayers? Why do you think this is so? (There is no "right" answer.)

Equal. Past, present, and the future each represent a different aspect of the same time. One isn't more important than the other, but you can only understand one alongside the others. You cannot, for example, understand the past without also knowing about both the present and the future. Suppose you went to church on Sunday. On the next day, Monday, you can say that your going to church happened in the past. How do you know it was in the past? Because you know it is an event that happened before the present day, Monday. You see, you know the past only in relation to the present. The same is true for the future. All times—present, past, and the future—are equal and are known only in relation to the other. This represents their *equality*. In the same way, God the Father, God the Son, and God the Holy Spirit are equal persons as One God. The way we understand the Son, for example, helps us understand the Father and the Holy Spirit, too.

Coeternal means the Father, the Son, and the Holy Spirit have existed, and will exist, together at creation and for all time.

Coeternal. We can't really understand the time without a past, present, and future—those three elements are **coeternal**. That is, all three are part of one; they have been so always and together will always be a part of our concept of time. The Son and the Holy Spirit were with God the Father before creation, are with God now, and will be with God to the end of time. In much the same way, the three persons, God the Father, God the Son, and God the Holy Spirit, have existed and will exist together for all time.

Activity: Read the closing to Paul's second letter to the Corinthians (2 Corinthians 13:13). What is Paul saying about how God the Father, God the Son, and God the Holy Spirit is working in our lives?

What the Words in the Apostles' Creed Mean

With a closer look at the meaning of the Trinity, we can begin to explore each part of the Apostles' Creed. Let's start with the most basic statement of belief.

I believe in God

Three intertwined circles represent the equality, unity, and coeternal nature of the three persons of the Trinity.

We begin with the first person of the Trinity—God, the Father. We're affirming that God is real, that there is a wonderful and magnificent "other" to whom we're faithful, in whom we trust, and who is intimately concerned with each of us—our well-being and our relationships with other people and all creation. But even more than that, we're proclaiming that we love God, we give our hearts to God, and we want to have a relationship with him.

the Father almighty,
creator of heaven and earth.

We don't believe in just any God. The God we love adopted us as his children and enters human history again and again with mighty acts that always make our friendship with him stronger. We believe in the God who made all things, both in heaven and on earth. We believe in the God who is the source of all things, everywhere.

God as Father is just one image that Christians use to express their experience of God. Throughout the Bible, God is described in many ways. God is described as both male and female. In Isaiah 66:13, for example, God is depicted as a mother who comforts her child. God is described as nature. In Psalm 28, for example, the psalmist calls God "my Rock." The prayers we use during church services express many images for God: God as ruler of the universe, fountain of life, source of goodness, holy Lord, shield and armor of light, holy wisdom, and giver of life. These images acknowledge that God reveals God's self in many ways. Any one image cannot adequately describe God.

Acknowledging God—and our loving relationship with him—makes us see the world in a totally different way. When the Israelites faced a hostile wilderness as they journeyed out of Egypt and wondered how they'd ever find their way, God guided them with a cloud by day and a pillar of fire by night. When they had nothing to eat, God gave them manna from heaven—enough for their daily needs. When they were thirsty, God led them to a rock that Moses struck ordering it to gush with water to quench their thirst.

> Believing in God changes the world from threatening and hostile to a world of hope and promise.

In the Christian Scriptures, Jesus continued to show us new ways of seeing the world. The poor, he said, will receive the kingdom of God, the hungry will be satisfied, the sad will laugh, and those who mourn will be comforted. When we see the world the way Jesus sees it, we look at the world a lot differently. Later in the chapter, we'll explore how believing in God changes our actions.

I believe in Jesus Christ, his only Son, our Lord.

We proclaim our belief in the second person of the Trinity—Jesus Christ. By saying "I believe in Jesus Christ," we're doing more than acknowledging that somebody named Jesus lived in a little country in the Middle East two thousand years ago. Instead, we're committing our lives to this Jesus and becoming his followers, or disciples. We're committing ourselves to the law of Moses (the Ten Commandments) and to the new commandment of Jesus: to love our neighbor as ourselves.

The second part of this phrase (his only Son) affirms that Jesus is the perfect human image of the Divine. Just as we reflect our own parents, Jesus reflected God. His life and ministry show us the essence of God, which is love. We call Jesus "our Lord" because we know he brings us to God. In the Gospel according to John, Jesus says, "I am the way, and the truth, and the life. No one comes to the Father except through me" (John 14:6).

He was conceived by the power of the Holy Spirit
and born of the Virgin Mary.

This is a strong statement! It says that we believe Jesus is both human and divine. By entering our world as a human being, God entered history and became a person just like you and me. Jesus was born, just like us, into a human family, and grew up in that family, first as a child, then as a teenager, and finally into an adult.

The gospels focus on Jesus' public ministry as an adult and don't say very much at all about Jesus' youth. This shouldn't surprise us. The gospels aren't modern biographies. They are proclamations of the good news that God's kingdom is near.

But the gospels do tell us lots of things about what Jesus was like. Like us, Jesus slept, ate, laughed, and cried. Like us, Jesus faced temptations. Like us, Jesus faced times of weakness and asked God to take away his troubles. Like us, Jesus needed his closest friends for support. Like us, Jesus felt pain. Jesus was subjected to the greatest suffering we can imagine—death on the cross.

Our belief that Jesus was God in the flesh is called the **incarnation**. That means that God took on a human identity to live as one of us to help us see and believe that God is the ruler of all things. We say the words "Virgin Mary" both to emphasize Jesus' humanity and to connect Jesus with the ancient prophecy in Isaiah 7:14: "Therefore the Lord himself will give you a sign. Look, the young woman is with child and shall bear a son, and shall name him Immanuel [meaning God is with us]".

Did You Know?

The gospel writers based their writings on a Greek version of this Hebrew verse, which translated the word "young" as "virgin." The word "virgin" tells that it was God's will to enter the world as one of us.

Activity: In the section "God the Son" in the Catechism in the Book of Common Prayer, find and report the answer to this question: Why did Jesus take our human nature?

Jesus was also fully divine. Nothing separated Jesus from God. Jesus expressed the love of God in his life by healing the sick, forgiving sins, mending broken relationships, turning away from evil, and calling everyone back to friendship with God. We don't mean that Jesus was just a man who led a good life, but that God the Father lived completely in Jesus the person. God took on human nature in Jesus.

He suffered under Pontius Pilate,

At first it might seem odd to mention Pontius Pilate in a statement of belief about God. Pilate got a bad rap in the Bible as the Roman leader who questioned Jesus at his trial and condemned him to death on the cross. So why do we include him in our creed? Mentioning Pontius Pilate by name sets Jesus squarely into human history. Pontius Pilate was governor of Judea, an ancient region in Palestine that was part of the Roman Empire and from 26 to 36 C.E., the time of Jesus' crucifixion, included the city of Jerusalem. His rule is recorded by the Jewish historian Josephus, who lived shortly after Jesus.

was crucified, died, and was buried.
He descended to the dead.

Jesus really did suffer and die as a human on the cross. Through Jesus, God chose to suffer and die as one of us. We say he descended to the dead not necessarily to say that Jesus literally went to a place where the dead resided, but that God offers salvation through Jesus to all people—to the living and those who had already died before Jesus came to the earth. Death is not the last word for anyone. God offers freedom from death, or salvation, to *all* people.

On the third day he rose again.

After Jesus died, a number of women who were followers of Jesus came to the tomb where Jesus was laid to anoint his body with perfumes and oils. But they were amazed to find that the tomb was empty. An angel appeared and told the women that Jesus had risen from the dead, or resurrected. The women ran to tell Jesus' closest friends, the disciples. For forty days, the risen Jesus revealed himself to the disciples, who recognized him whenever they shared a meal together.

The names of the women who went to the tomb are different in each gospel. Matthew, Mark, and John all mention Mary Magdalene by name.

By conquering death, Jesus opened for the way of eternal life. "Eternal life and salvation" has a variety of meanings. Eternal life and salvation means a life without physical or emotional suffering and a life where our sins are forgiven. We cannot experience salvation completely as human beings living on earth. But through our faith in God and with God's help we can make choices that lessen human suffering and demonstrate God's love to others.

The resurrection of Jesus is at the heart of what it means to be a Christian. Through Jesus' resurrection we are made a new creation and given the way of eternal life.

Because Jesus rose from the dead, we no longer have to live completely separated from God. And just as he revealed himself to the disciples, Jesus continues to reveal himself to us through the Eucharist, the meal Christians share together, and through the loving actions of people toward one another and creation. Death did not end the story.

He ascended into heaven,
and is seated at the right hand of the Father.

We believe that Jesus dwells with the Father just as someday we will, too. The words "seated at the right hand" don't mean that Jesus is literally sitting next to God on God's right. It is a way of saying that Jesus shares in the authority and power of God as ruler of all creation.

Activity: Look at the Calendar of the Church Year in the Book of Common Prayer. On what day do we celebrate that Jesus returned to the Father in heaven?

He will come again to judge the living and the dead.

Jesus came to proclaim the good news of God: "The time is fulfilled, and the kingdom of God has come near; repent, and believe in the good news" (Mark 1:15). God created the world and rules the world today. What we mean by ruling the world is that God has a purpose and order for the world. We are to love our neighbors as ourselves. We are to take care of the earth and all living creatures. God sent Jesus to show us the way to live according to God's will and to offer the healing we need to love ourselves, others, and creation. We also look forward to when we are no longer separated from God and we are completely within God's will. We look for the time when our relationship with God is completely restored, when we meet God face-to-face, so to speak.

I believe in the Holy Spirit,

The descending dove is a symbol of the Holy Spirit. Three gospels mention the Holy Spirit descending as a dove on Jesus at his baptism.

The **Holy Spirit** is the third person of the Trinity—God's power and presence in our past, our present, and our future.

The Holy Spirit is God at work in the world and the church—from the beginning of time to eternity. The Holy Spirit is the breath over nothingness at creation, the manna from heaven that fed the Israelites in the wilderness, the words of God at the start of Jesus' ministry saying, "This is my Son, the Beloved, with whom I am well pleased" (Matthew 3:17). The Holy Spirit is the rush of violent wind at Pentecost when the apostles began to spread the good news of Jesus in other languages. The Holy Spirit is the person of the Trinity that strengthens, nourishes, and sustains you and me. Through the Holy Spirit, we live in Christ and Christ lives in us. Through the Holy Spirit, we bring Christ's joy, peace, and justice into the world.

the holy catholic Church,

"Catholic" is another word for universal, or worldwide. When we say that we believe in the **catholic** Church, we mean we support one universal faith community, all those who believe in Jesus. This church began with Jesus. It was founded when the Holy Spirit descended upon the apostles on Pentecost. And it continues today. We, like those baptized at the founding of the church, devote ourselves "to the apostles' teaching and fellowship, to the breaking of bread, and to the prayers" (Acts 2:42).

The word "saints" with a lowercase "s" means the community of faithful people who believe in God and Jesus Christ. This is different from the uppercase "S" Saints who are given particular honor in the Roman Catholic Church for their devout lives and miracles.

the communion of saints,

We are each one of many members of the body of Christ. The word "saints" here means a community of faithful people who believe in God and Jesus Christ. When we are initiated into the life of the church at baptism, we become a saint with a lowercase "s."

Affirming our membership in this community means that we're related in our faith with all other members of the body of Christ, or the church. We care for that relationship through worship, prayer, and serving one another.

the forgiveness of sins,

No matter what we do wrong, God wants to restore our friendship and forgives us even before we ask. At baptism, we—or our parents and sponsors—renounce evil and turn to Jesus Christ as our Savior. But inevitably, we miss the mark and fail to live up to our baptismal promises by the things we do—and by the things we don't do. Our actions bring evil into the world, and sometimes we fail to do what God asks us. So again and again, we need to turn away from evil, say we're sorry, and ask for God's forgiveness. We can be confident that God will always forgive us.

the resurrection of the body, and the life everlasting.

We believe that God will raise us in our entirety to a new life with God. Because we are living members of the body of Christ—the church—we share in Jesus' resurrection. Just as Jesus conquered sin, suffering, and death, we will no longer experience pain or suffering. We will be resurrected in perfection by God and, as resurrected people, we will be united with God, living in perfect joy and peace with one another, loving God and each other in a way that is not possible now. Ultimately, nothing—not sin, not suffering that we know now on earth, not even death—will separate us from the love of God.

FAITH AS SEEING AND RESPONDING

Bartimaeus's faith opened up his eyes and made him jump up and follow Jesus. Notice those two actions: faith gave sight and sight prompted a response. The same is true for our faith. Our faith means we see the world within a relationship with God. And we respond in ways that maintain our relationship with God and the world. Like Bartimaeus, we're called to follow.

We say we believe in—give our hearts to—God almighty. What we see is a God who is with us, loves us, and takes care of us. God is at the center of our lives and we promise to live according to God's will. We say we believe in—give our hearts to—Jesus. What we see is a world in which God knows us intimately—our pain, our joy, and our fears—because through Jesus, he became one of us. Jesus still shows us signs of the kingdom of

God that is filled with life, joy, plenty, and justice. In return, we promise to be disciples of Jesus—to be signs of the kingdom of God today. We say we believe in—give our hearts to—the Holy Spirit. That means we see a world in which God is actively offering us forgiveness, giving us what we need to grow, and guiding us to make good choices. We respond by welcoming God's guidance, accepting God's forgiveness, and seeking God's will for our lives. We do this by taking the time to pray each day, offering God our questions, and asking for guidance. We do this by inviting God into our decisions and continuing to ask ourselves whether what we are doing is sharing the love that God gives us.

Believing changes how we see things and how we respond to the world. Belief without action is not belief.

How Do We Know How to Respond?

Remember, our relationship with God is a covenant relationship. The stories of the Hebrew Scriptures (Old Testament), the life and ministry of Jesus, and the promises we made at baptism tell us about how to live into that sacred covenant. When God started a covenant with the Israelites, he promised to be their God, guiding them and giving them land, food, and drink. In response, God required his people to be faithful, to love justice, to do mercy, and to walk humbly with their God. Christians refer to the sacred covenant God established with the Israelites as the **Old Covenant**.

As part of the covenant with the Israelites, God gave the Ten Commandments to show what it means to live within the covenant. You can read them in Exodus 20:1–17 and also in Deuteronomy 5:6–21. The first four commandments define our relationship with God. We worship one God. We honor God through love and respect and by putting him first. The last six commandments define our relationship with others. To be faithful to our relationships, with others means we act in ways that show honor, love, and respect for all life.

Activity: The Ten Commandments, also known as the Decalogue, are given on pages 317 and 350 of the Book of Common Prayer. The Decalogue is an option as part of the service, "A Penitential Order." Why do you think this is so?

Jesus came into the world to fulfill the laws that God gave to the Israelites. That is, Jesus fulfilled God's laws by perfectly loving God and loving his neighbors as he loved himself. And more, through his resurrection, Jesus fulfilled the laws by offering us forgiveness for all the times we disobey God's laws. Jesus started a new covenant—a new relationship for us with God. In the **New Covenant**, Jesus promises us the kingdom of God—a life marked by joy, community, plenty, and justice. In the New Covenant, Christ calls us to respond in love by keeping his laws, especially the following two **Great Commandments**:

> *"You shall love the Lord your God with all your heart, and with all your soul, and with all your mind."*
>
> and
>
> *"You shall love your neighbor as yourself."* (Matthew 22:37–39)

Notice how these two Great Commandments follow the Ten Commandments. The first commandment is about loving God while the second is about loving others. To live within the covenant relationship with God, our every action should reflect our love for God, self, and neighbor. The Catechism in the Book of Common Prayer (847) offers a specific guide on how to do this.

Honoring our relationship with God means that we

- love and obey God and bring others to know him;
- put nothing in the place of God;
- show God respect in thought, word, and deed;
- and set aside regular times for worship, prayer, and the study of God's ways.

We choose to take these actions as free responses to our loving God. Imagine meeting a person who brings out the best in you, makes you laugh, and who stays by your side when you really need a friend. We introduce that friend to our other friends, and always make time to hang out together.

These first four actions place God at the center of our lives. They help us to know God's generous love. Knowing that love, we can see the goodness that God wants for the world. By taking time to love God and putting God at the center, we allow God to draw us toward actions that share God's love. These actions will be to:

- love, honor, and help our neighbors;
- respect life and do things that bring peace to the world;

- respect ourselves and our bodies;
- be honest and fair in all that we do;
- speak the truth;
- honor the life and gifts of others.

God loves all of creation. When we join God's kingdom, we also love all creation as God loves us—without reservation. We take care of the earth and everything in it. We live honestly. We usually think of rules as a nuisance, but they're really a way of freedom because they help people live happily with one another. The Old Covenant and the New Covenant show us the way to have good relationships with God and with others.

Sin is seeking our own will instead of the will of God, thus distorting our relationship with God.

Breaking Relationship

Following God's will isn't always easy. Sometimes we fall short of doing God's will. That is, we **sin**. The Catechism defines sin as "seeking of our own will instead of the will of God, thus distorting our relationship with God, with other people, and with all creation" (Book of Common Prayer, 848).

We cannot promise not to sin, but we can promise to acknowledge when we have acted wrongly, seek forgiveness, and with God's help promise to make right choices.

When we sin we are breaking our promises to God and our relationship with God and one another. We often put ourselves—not God—first. Every day, things that are bad tempt us away from the love of God. This evil takes away our faith and takes away our ability to know God's love and see the possibilities for a world filled with God's love.

Asking for Forgiveness

What if we break our promises to God and one another? At our baptism, we—or our parents and godparents—promised "to persevere in resisting evil, and whenever you fall into sin, repent and return to the Lord." We didn't promise to be perfect or never to sin—that would be a promise we could never keep. We promised that when we sin we'd acknowledge what we'd done, turn away from sin, and turn toward God by asking forgiveness from God and those we've hurt. We promised to restore a right relationship with God and with other people. We can seek forgiveness in lots of

A "right relationship" is one in which our choices fulfill God's will for us.

ways. We can ask God's forgiveness any time at all. We also confess our sins as a community during our Sunday worship. And we can receive the sacrament called Reconciliation of a Penitent, confessing our sins privately to a priest and receiving absolution, or forgiveness. Chapter 6 explores this sacrament.

PUTTING YOUR FAITH INTO PRACTICE

Like Bartimaeus, we see the world in a whole new way when our eyes are opened up by faith. With our every action, we try to follow the two Great Commandments of Jesus, and our baptismal promises help us do that. Your confirmation class and this text will help you discover ways to fulfill these promises by exploring the Bible, the history of the church, worship, prayer, and ministry. Our actions are the ways we put into practice the faith that's in our hearts.

Chapter 5

Worship: Responding to God's Blessings

Then God said, "Let us make humankind in our image, according to our likeness." (Genesis 1:26a)

In the beginning, God was extremely busy. He brought order out of chaos by separating the heavens from the earth, the dry land from the sea, and light from the darkness. God said let the trees and plants grow and bear beautiful flowers, fruit, and seeds. God filled the earth with living creatures of every kind—birds that fly, insects that creep, and monsters of the sea. God looked it over and saw that it was good. And on the sixth day, he made humans and blessed them. God looked at all creation and thought, "This is *really* good." Imagine that! Immediately after God created us humans, God blessed us. God continues to bless us each and every day. We respond to these blessings by worshipping God.

What do we mean—worship God? Suppose your family gets together for your birthday. It's a day dedicated to celebrating *you*. Your parents, grandparents, and favorite relatives and friends give you gifts they've chosen with care and presented with joy. You unwrap your packages slowly, with great anticipation—or you tear into them eagerly. And underneath the pretty paper, you find the gifts you'd been hoping for—the gifts that tell you that your family and friends know you and want you to be happy. That's bound to make you feel good inside—and those good feelings probably pour out into thank-you's and great big hugs.

Worship is a lot like those hugs and thank-you's. It's a response of praise and thanksgiving to the God who created us, knows us, blesses us each day, and wants to fulfill our heart's desires. We respond by giving our love and our thanks. As people created by God, it's our very nature to draw close to our creator. That's what worship is all about.

Worship is our response of praise and thanksgiving to the God who creates us, blesses us, and loved us.

One of my favorite stories in the Hebrew Scriptures is about God's promise to Abraham and Sarah: Their descendants, he told them, would be as numerous as the stars. As a child I'd often lie outside in the backyard looking up at the vast, dark sky. So many stars! How could someone have that many descendants? Especially Abraham and Sarah—when God made that promise they were already pretty old and still hadn't had a single baby. But Abraham believed. He must have—after all, he left his family and friends and the safety of his hometown for the wilderness and a very unlikely promise.

We may not have a picture of God, but from the story of Abraham and Sarah and other stories in the Bible, we get a pretty good idea what he is like. This story tells us that God is bigger than all the stars in the sky, and that God's love makes everything possible. Looking at the stars as a child, I was filled with a sense of God's infinite love. And I was grateful. Abraham and Sarah also had thankful hearts. On the long and difficult journey in the wilderness, Abraham took the time to build altars—piles of stones—to remember God's presence and to offer praise and thanksgiving. This image—of Abraham and Sarah stopping on their journey or in the middle of a busy day to offer thanks—can help us through our own life's journey.

Activity: Look up Genesis 12:7 and Genesis 13:18. Abram (later called Abraham) built altars along his journey. To what or to whom was Abram responding?

Just as he did with Abraham and Sarah, God blesses us and calls us on our own journey, promising great things. When we see God acting in our lives, we respond naturally as they did, by offering thanks and praise. Worshipping God can be as simple as lighting a candle at home and saying a few words that tell God of our love and thankfulness. Or on Sunday we can gather to worship with God's people.

THE BOOK OF COMMON PRAYER

In the Book of Common Prayer we find a lot of ways to worship. The **Book of Common Prayer** is the manual for personal and community worship in the Episcopal Church. It has the services and prayers for worship. We call the services that we do together—Holy Eucharist, baptism, confirmation, and so on—liturgies. The word "liturgy" comes from a Greek word that means work done for the sake of others. **Liturgy** is the work of the Christian people and includes words, actions, vestments, scriptures, and prayers. It's not something we watch; liturgies are truly the work and words of all the people.

Liturgies are powerful. They express our beliefs, and help us understand them. Consider Holy Communion. When the priest gives us the communion bread and says, "The Body of Christ, the bread of heaven," and we respond, "Amen," we become part of the event that we are celebrating. We are participating in the sacrifice that Jesus offered to God and to the world. We, like Jesus, are offering ourselves to God and to the world. How do we make that offering? With our whole selves—by the way we act towards others and what we offer the world. The bread and the wine also nourish us. We leave the table strengthened to act like Jesus in the world.

Holy Communion is the part of the service when the priest takes, blesses, breaks, and shares the bread as the body of Christ and shares the wine as the blood of Christ.

Week after week, we repeat the beautiful words and actions of liturgy. And each time we return to the communion table, we bring along the experience of living like Jesus—being the body of Christ—all week long. We're fed again for our journey, and our desire to do the work of Jesus is nurtured, too.

Sometimes our Episcopal liturgies can seem pretty complicated. The Book of Common Prayer has rules and directions for lots of services—more than two dozen of them. Check out page 13 for a rundown of the major services. You'll find a similar page before most services, explaining what the service is about and giving instructions, or **rubrics**, for doing it. "The Calendar of the Church Year" (pages 15–33) lists the important days and seasons of the church year.

Rubrics are directions for ceremonies. The word "rubric" comes from the Latin word rubrica, which means red ochre. In early manuscripts liturgical instructions were written in red ink.

The church year is the calendar of liturgical seasons that begins with Advent and continues with Christmas, Epiphany, Lent, Easter, and Pentecost.

Activity: Read "Concerning the Service of the Church" in the Book of Common Prayer. What are the regular services appointed for regular public worship in the Episcopal Church? Who normally leads these services? What happens when that person(s) is not present?

The Book of Common Prayer is a treasure chest of our faith. Besides the liturgies, it also contains one complete book of the Hebrew Scriptures—Psalms, prayers of praise and thanksgiving for many occasions, an outline of the faith, historical documents of the church, tables to find the date of Easter and other holy days, and a list of readings from the Bible for services throughout the church year. The activities in this book introduce you to all the amazing treasures of the Book of Common Prayer.

HOLY EUCHARIST

> *So those who welcomed his message were baptized, and that day about three thousand persons were added. They devoted themselves to the apostles' teaching and fellowship, to the breaking of the bread and the prayers.* (Acts 2:41–42)

In our most important act of worship, **Holy Eucharist**, we follow the example of the first Christians as we learn about God (teaching), care for one another (fellowship), receive communion (breaking of the bread), and join together in prayer. We celebrate Eucharist on Sundays and other major feast days, such as Christmas and Ash Wednesday. Eucharist is also called the Lord's Supper, Holy Communion, and Mass. Many Christians celebrate Eucharist every day. The word "Eucharist" comes from the Greek word *Eucharistia*, meaning "the giving of thanks." In the Eucharist we remember the life, death, and resurrection of Jesus Christ and proclaim that we await his coming in glory. Through the Eucharist we're strengthened and nourished for our lives today and get a taste of what God has prepared for us in heaven. The Eucharist is a celebration by God's family of God's love for us.

"Mass" is another word for Holy Eucharist. It comes from the Latin word meaning "to send" and reminds us that communion prepares us for the work God has given us to do out in the world.

The format for worship has ancient roots. The Hebrew Scriptures, in Nehemiah 8, describes a service with readings from the law of Moses and a talk about the reading—a sermon—followed by a meal. Our service has similar parts: the Liturgy of the Word, when we listen to passages from the Bible, and the Liturgy of the Table, when we take, bless, break, and give the bread and wine of communion. The first Christians were Jews who believed in Jesus. They gathered in Jewish places of worship called synagogues. So, it's no surprise that the Eucharist is based on synagogue services.

LITURGY OF THE WORD

Our congregations are filled with all kinds of people with different jobs, different backgrounds, and different ways of looking at the world. But all of us come together to worship as the people of God. So to gather us as one, the Liturgy of the Word begins with a brief entrance rite, or ceremony, that focuses our minds and hearts toward God and one another as a community of faith. During the opening hymn, the leaders of the service—acolytes, choir, deacons, priests, and, when present, the bishop—process, or march, to the front of the church. They start at the back of the church and make their way through the people, all the way up to the altar—and that's important. It demonstrates our belief that worshipping God is the work of the people.

Once everyone is in their places, the celebrant continues with the **opening acclamation**, a greeting to God's family that proclaims in whose name we gather, and the collect for purity. Then we sing the **Gloria**, a song of praise to God. The entrance rite ends with a **collect**, a short prayer that "collects" the themes of the day.

Activity: The collects and other portions of the service are set by what are called Propers. These are the readings that belong to a particular Sunday. Look for the first page of the section in your Prayer Book entitled, "The Collects." What readings and prayers are set forth in the Propers?

We believe that God is present in both Word and Sacrament. Both nourish our lives as the people of God. The Liturgy of the Word feeds our minds and hearts by our reading passages of the Bible. This portion of the liturgy usually includes four readings: a reading from the Hebrew Scriptures, a psalm, a reading from the the Epistles, and a reading from the Gospels, the stories of the ministry of Jesus. The readings are based on a three-year cycle called the **lectionary**. In year A we read from the Gospel according to Matthew, year B from the Gospel of Mark, and year C from the Gospel of Luke. Readings from the Gospel of John are sprinkled throughout each of the three years, especially the year that we read the Gospel of Mark. The Epistles are read in sequence and the readings from the Hebrew Scriptures are related to either the Gospel

---

A collect has three parts: a call to God, a petition, and a conclusion. You might try writing a collect for grace one evening at supper. Use what happened to you that day to help you fill in the blanks: "Oh, God who ______" "I ask for_____" "So that____."

The lectionary is a cycle of readings for services throughout the church year.

---

or Epistle readings. During the season of Easter, readings from the Acts of the Apostles, one of the books of the Christian Scriptures, may take the place of the Hebrew Scripture reading. With a common lectionary, every Episcopal Church reads the same Scriptures on any given Sunday.

Because the lectionary has readings from the entire Bible, following the lectionary challenges us to understand the way God has worked throughout history, through events that are sometimes confusing and writings that sometimes contradict one another. We can't just stick to our favorite verses—the lectionary forces us to wrestle with different ways of understanding God and applying his Word to our lives. The reading from the Hebrew Scriptures reminds us that Christians and Jews share the same roots. The God of the Hebrew Scriptures is the same God as the one in the Christian Scriptures.

Someone from the congregation reads the Hebrew Scriptures and Epistle passages and a deacon or priest reads the gospel passage. The Gospel is the good news for the people of God, so the deacon or priest will often walk to a place within the congregation to read it. Sometimes, the congregation may sit silently for a few minutes after the Gospel has been read, and after that the priest interprets the readings in a sermon or homily, which helps us to grow from the Word of God—to help us understand the stories in the Bible and to make us think about how the lessons in the Bible teach us about how to live. After the sermon, we stand and profess our beliefs with the words of the Nicene Creed.

A short sermon is often called a homily.

The Universal Church refers to all Christian churches as a single body of Christ in the world.

Then it's time to offer intercessory prayers—to pray for the needs of others in the Prayers of the People. The Book of Common Prayer requires that the Prayers of the People cover these six areas:

- the Universal Church, its members, and its mission,
- the nation and all in authority,
- the welfare of the world,
- the concerns of the local community,
- those who suffer and those in any trouble, and
- the departed, or those who have died

During the prayers we also offer our thanksgivings—our thank-you's to God.

Activity: Rubrics, directions in the Book of Common Prayer, are written in italics. The rubrics in Morning Prayer tell us the posture for prayer. What posture is recommended?

The prayer book requires that when we come to the Eucharist, "we should examine our lives, repent of our sins and be in love and charity with all people" (Book of Common Prayer, 860). That means that before we receive Jesus, we need to say that we're sorry for the times we've disobeyed God and hurt other people. That's what we call seeking reconciliation. So at this part of the liturgy, we confess our sins against God and our neighbor. Because we fail to love God with our whole hearts and continually choose not to love our neighbors as ourselves, we always need God's mercy and forgiveness.

Reconciliation involves confessing your sins and receiving forgiveness.

After renewing our friendship with God and our neighbors, we exchange the peace. The exchange of peace comes from Jewish practices that required people to be reconciled with one another before offering a gift at the altar (see, for example, Matthew 5:23–24). The first thing the risen Jesus said when he appeared to the frightened disciples was, "Peace be with you" (John 20:19–21). It is the peace that the risen Jesus gives us that we share with one another. The peace ends the Liturgy of the Word.

LITURGY OF THE TABLE

> *Then he took a loaf of bread, and when he had given thanks, he broke it and gave it to them, saying, "This is my body, which is given for you. Do this in remembrance of me."* (Luke 22:19)

The Liturgy of the Table, or Holy Communion, is the climax of our liturgy. We do it in response to Jesus' command to the disciples at the Last Supper to "Do this in remembrance of me." We follow this commandment every time we celebrate communion by doing the same things Jesus did during his last meal with the disciples. We take the bread, give thanks to God, break the bread, and share it. We do this to remember Jesus' life on earth and his resurrection, and to announce that we expect that he will return.

The **Last Supper** refers to the meal that Jesus ate with his disciples on the evening before he was crucified on the cross.

But Holy Communion is more than remembering a past event. Every Eucharist is a new offering and sacrifice. Through the prayers at Eucharist and the Holy Spirit, the bread and drink the wine, become for us the body and blood of Christ. As we eat the bread and the wine we share in his offering and sacrifice. What does that mean? As we take Jesus into our bodies, we are strengthened by Jesus and through that strength offer ourselves to God and the world. We accept God's love into our bodies and offer ourselves out in the world. Our offerings are our relationships of love and our actions that demonstrate God's love for all people. The liturgy makes this clear to us with the prayer after we receive communion when we ask God to send us out into the world to love and serve him.

Take, Bless, Break, and Give

Jesus did four important things when he shared bread with the disciples and the Liturgy of the Table follows these four actions. Jesus *took bread, blessed it, broke it,* and *gave it.* When Jesus fed a crowd of five thousand people who had come to hear him preach (Matthew 14), he took five loaves of bread and two fish, blessed them, broke them, and gave them to the crowd—and it was enough to feed all those hungry people! In the gospel accounts of the Last Supper, Jesus did the same four things—taking, blessing, breaking, and giving the bread. And after he rose from the dead, the disciples recognized Jesus by these same four actions—take, bless, break, and give—each time he appeared to them. The Liturgy of the Table begins with the first action—taking.

Paten and Chalice.

Take

We begin by gathering gifts from among the people and taking them to the altar to present them as an offering to God and the church. By presenting our gifts of bread and wine, music, and money, we *return* the blessings that God gave us—the blessings of creation and our labor. Our labor transforms grapes into wine and wheat into bread. Because God is the giver of all things,

The formal name for the offering of gifts is the offertory.

ultimately they are gifts that we *return* to God. During the offertory, the deacon or priest sets the altar table for communion. He or she spreads a white square cloth called the **corporal** on the altar, brings the bread on a plate called a **paten**, and pours the wine and some water into a **chalice**. One chalice is usually placed on the altar, showing that we share *one* bread and *one* wine in communion.

Give Thanks

The second main action is to return the blessings, or thank God, for all that he has given us. The **Great Thanksgiving** begins with a dialogue between the celebrant and the people. We ask God to be with us, and we lift our hearts and give thanks to God in the words of the **Sursum corda** ("Lift up your hearts. We lift them to the Lord"). The congregation joins with all the angels in heaven and all the people on earth to sing praise to God in the **Sanctus** (Holy, holy, holy Lord . . .").

Sursum corda is Latin for "hearts upward." *Sanctus* means "holy."

We continue our thanksgiving by remembering the gift of creation and God's saving acts throughout history—the covenant established with Abraham and Sarah and the life, death, and resurrection of Jesus. We thank God for his mighty works and his enduring care for us. We also recall the Last Supper and the **words of institution** Jesus gave us: "Take, eat: This is my Body which is given for you. Do this for the remembrance of me." The words of institution are addressed not to the congregation, but to God. It is important to remember that this is not a re-enactment of the Last Supper, but a prayer to God. After the priest has said these words, all of us respond by proclaiming the greatest mystery of our faith, the **memorial acclamation**:

Christ has died.
Christ is risen.
Christ will come again.

The bread and the wine are made holy (consecrated) by the prayers of all the people present. A priest alone cannot consecrate bread and wine.

In all Episcopal Eucharistic prayers, the person leading the Eucharist, usually a priest, asks God to send the Holy Spirit to make the bread and the wine holy so that it will be the body and blood of Jesus Christ. This is called the **epiclesis**. The celebrant has no special powers. In fact, a priest cannot consecrate bread and wine alone. It is through the prayers of all present—the congregation and clergy alike—and through God's blessings that the bread and wine, are made holy and become the body and blood of Christ. We believe that Christ is present in the bread and the wine and this presence nourishes us and heals us. By partaking in the bread and the wine, we are strengthened to serve God in the world.

Activity: What are the words of the epiclesis in Eucharistic Prayer A?

After the Great Thanksgiving and before the Breaking of the Bread, together we say the Lord's Prayer. The Lord's Prayer reminds us that we are asked to bring God's kingdom to the here-and-now, that God will give us what we need to fulfill God's will, and that we need to ask for forgiveness.

Break

Following the Great Thanksgiving, the celebrant breaks the bread to distribute it among the people, just as Jesus broke the bread to distribute among the disciples. During the breaking of the bread, the congregation sings the **fraction anthem**.

The word fraction comes from a Latin word that means "to break." The fraction anthem gets its name from marking the breaking of the bread.

Give

Right after the breaking of the bread, the people are invited to the altar table to receive both the bread and the wine. In the Episcopal Church, all people who are baptized as Christians regardless of what particular church they were baptized in are welcome to take communion. The congregation comes forward together because we are one people partaking in one body of Christ. Taking communion is also intensely personal. As we eat the bread and drink the wine, we are each individually nourished in a real way by Christ's presence and healing grace in our lives.

Go Out

The final part of Holy Eucharist proclaims our going out. Unlike all other prayers in the service, here we proclaim our readiness to go out into the world to love and to serve God. Nourished with the body and blood of Christ, we're ready to do God's work in the world.

Our worship together shapes who we are. This might sound a little strange, but what we say and how we use our bodies during worship affects what we think. It really does. When we bow as the cross passes, we are submitting and giving respect to Jesus who died on the cross. So, our bodies connect the cross with bowing and through bowing with submission. By worshipping in a community we experience God with other people. This experience shapes our belief that God is known in community. Each part of our worship shapes our belief. The Liturgy of the Word tells us stories about God's saving acts for us in history and how to apply them to our lives today. Together, we affirm our faith and pray for others. In the Liturgy of the Table, we remember Christ's death and resurrection and take part in a sacred meal. When we come together to worship each Sunday in these two parts of the liturgy, we continue the actions of the first members of the church: "They devoted themselves to the apostles' teaching and fellowship, to the breaking of the bread, and the prayers" (Acts 2:42).

The Latin saying *"lex orandi, lex credendi,"* reflects our understanding that how we worship shapes what we believe.

THE MANY PEOPLE IN WORSHIP

All the members of the church participate in worship through song, prayer, giving thanks, and receiving communion. God made each of us different, with different gifts to contribute to worship. Below, I list several of the ways the ministers of the church use their gifts to help with worship.

Acolyte Anyone, often a young person, who helps in the service in a variety of ways, including lighting the candles, carrying the cross and candles in a procession, and assisting in setting the table. Acolytes also carry incense. Acolytes sometimes wear white albs or white cottas over colored cassocks.

Acolytes help in the service by carrying the cross and candles in the procession and assisting the bishop, priest, or deacon to set the table. Acolytes also carry incense.

Celebrant, also Presider The bishop or priest who presides at the Eucharist. Deacons may also serve as celebrants when the elements have already been consecrated. The celebrant, also called Presider, often wears a white alb and a stole during the Liturgy of the Word and puts a decorated chasuble, a loose-fitting garment that looks a little like a poncho, over the alb during the Liturgy of the Table.

Choir member A lay minister who leads sung music during worship. Choirs often sing anthems as musical offerings during the offertory. Choir members often wear robes.

Deacon A deacon is a person who has been ordained for a ministry of serving others, especially those in need. Deacons also have particular roles in worship. Because of their ministry of service, a deacon should read the Gospel and may lead the Prayers of the People. Deacons set the table and help to give the people the bread and the wine.

When a deacon is present at worship, he or she reads the Gospel, sets the table, and may lead the Prayers of the People.

Eucharistic minister A person who helps the priest or deacon give people the bread and wine of communion.

Readers The Prayers of the People and the lessons are generally led by someone from the congregation. Deacons may also lead the Prayers of the People. The one who reads the lesson is called a lector and is appointed by the clergy.

Verger A lay minister who directs in the processions of liturgy. The verger usually wears in a black cassock and carries a rod called a verge.

In Chapter 9 you'll learn to figure out—or discern—how you can use your gifts in worship and in the world to proclaim God's kingdom.

Activity: Who may bless the people at the conclusion of Holy Eucharist?

When we worship together, we gather in one place, sometimes with just one other person and sometimes with thousands of others. Sometimes we gather outdoors, but most times inside buildings. We call the building where we gather for worship a church.

THE CHURCH

The church isn't just a physical place—it's much greater than stone, bricks, and mortar. The Catechism tells us, "The church is the community of the New Covenant." So during the Prayers of the People, when we pray for *the church*, we're actually praying for the community of baptized members—all the people of God.

Activity: Look at the section "The Church" in the Catechism. Through whom does the church carry out its mission?

We use the word "church" to mean a community just as the writers of Acts and the Epistles did. The word for church in Greek, the language of the Gospels, Acts, and the Epistles, is *ekklesia*, which means "called out." For example, in the letter to the Colossians, Jesus is called the head of the body, the *ekklesia*—the community of people who believe in the risen Christ.

Buildings we call churches are sacred places Christians have set aside for worship. Since the very beginning, Christians have found places to gather. Two Gospels (Luke and John) tell us that until the day of Pentecost, the disciples gathered in the room where they saw Jesus after his resurrection. As members of the Jewish community, they also continued to pray and to teach in synagogues and the Temple until it was destroyed in 70 C.E. As Christianity spread and grew apart from Judaism, believers met in houses that they converted into places of worship. Sometimes, when the government persecuted Christians, they met in catacombs, hollowed-out tunnels used for burial. The earliest known complete church is a mid-third-century Roman house that was converted into a gathering place for Christians in a city in present-day Syria. It included a pool close to the entrance, which was likely used for baptism, and a reception area further in the house with a table around which the community broke bread. This design is similar to the design of churches today—a baptismal font near the entrance and a raised sanctuary with an altar for the Liturgy of the Table.

> Early Christians met in private homes.

The typical pattern of Christian churches today began in the fourth century, after Roman Emperor Constantine issued the Edict of Milan, which ended the persecution of Christians. Unlike the Jewish Temple or temples of Greek gods, Christian churches weren't meant as dwelling places for a god, but as central meeting places for the followers of Jesus. Churches built in the fourth century followed the design of Roman government meeting halls, called basilicas. These basilicas were rectangular, with a curved apse for a throne at which trials were held. We can trace much of our church furnishings to the early church and to the Roman government buildings of the fourth century.

The drawing on the right illustrates the layout of a typical Episcopal church today. Notice the curved apse from the Roman basilica. The rectangle of the basilica grew into a cross shape when architects in the eleventh century added two rooms—one for the priests and another for the remains of the dead—on either side of the central hall. The cross is comprised of three main areas: the nave, transept, and chancel. The **nave** is the vertical portion of the church where worshippers gather. The **chancel**, also called the sanctuary, contains the pulpit, lectern, and altar; it's often higher than the seats of the congregation and separated from the nave by a rail or screen. The **altar**, within the sanctuary, is the table around which Holy Communion is celebrated. The altar represents the presence of God and is the focus of our worship, so it's situated at the head of the cross. Often, churches are designed so that the congregation faces the east—the direction of the rising sun and a symbol of the risen Christ. In these churches, the altar is in the eastern-most part of the church. The **transept** is the horizontal part of the church extending from the nave and chancel. The transept typically contains chapels for more private prayer and worship.

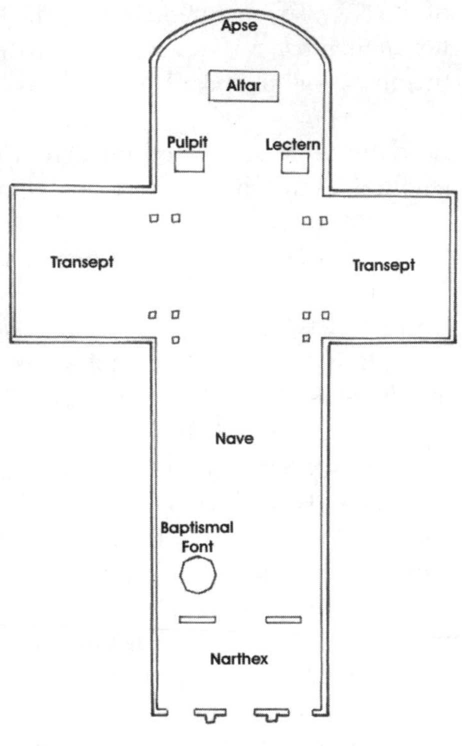

Cruciform Church

The word "nave" comes from the Latin word *navis,* meaning ship. A ship is an early symbol of the church.

Because baptism is the initiation rite into the membership of the church, a **baptismal font** or pool is usually close to the entrance of the church. It is close to the entrance to remind us that baptism is the rite of initiation into the church. Baptism is how we enter the church. The cathedral of St. John the Divine in New York City (stjohndivine.org) and our National Cathedral in Washington, D.C. (cathedral.org), are cross-shaped churches.

The drawing here illustrates another church design. In this circular layout, the altar is the central place around which people gather. This simple design returns to the layout of the synagogues and Temple familiar to people at the time of Jesus—and it's probably closer to the worship spaces of early Christians than the cross-shaped churches. This design highlights that everybody takes part in the liturgy. Baptismal fonts are usually just inside the main entrance or opposite the pulpit. St. Gregory's, San Francisco, California (saintgregorys.org), is built in a circular pattern.

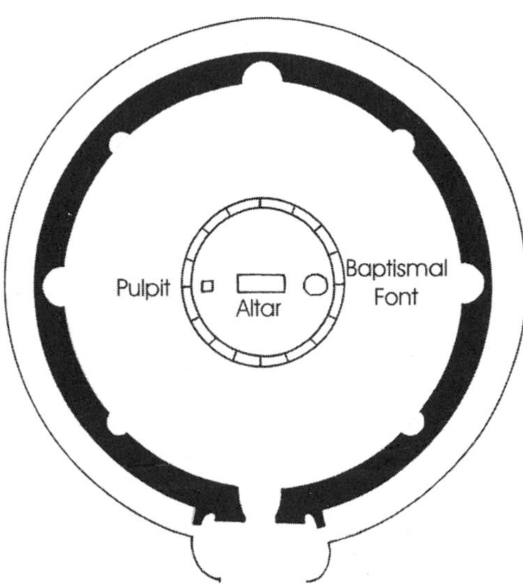

Circular Church Design

No matter how your church is designed, it provides a sacred space for celebrating the Liturgy of the Word and the Liturgy of the Table. The Liturgy of the Word takes place nearer to the people. The Hebrew Scriptures and Epistle readings are generally read from the lectern at the front of the nave on the side opposite the pulpit, which is where the Gospel is sometimes read and the sermon is preached. The Liturgy of the Table moves the central action toward the altar table, where the bread and wine are consecrated and received by those worshipping together.

The lectern and pulpit are also known as an ambo.

People have been building sacred places for worshipping God since ancient times. Remember, Abraham and Sarah created stone altars to worship at the roadside. The Israelites built a tabernacle, or portable church, so God would be with them wherever they went. The Israelites built the Temple at Jerusalem. Muslims have mosques and Jews have synagogues. Christians have churches. We worship in other places, too—around the evening supper table when we say grace together, on a mountaintop when we thank God for creation, and when we set aside time in a quiet place in our homes to pray and meditate on God's Word. We can even worship in cyberspace. At geraniumfarm.org, for

You can say prayers at geraniumfarm.org and dailyoffice.org.

example, you can light a candle and offer a prayer. At dailyoffice.org you can say the Daily Office. Pray-as-you-go.org has meditations as mp3 files.

Symbols of Worship

Have you ever smelled fresh-baked bread or pie at home? Your mouth begins to water. You turn the corner into the kitchen almost expecting see your family gathered around the table as they have many times before. That one smell fills us with happy memories and a sense of gratitude. Worship is similar. When we enter a church and see familiar symbols of Jesus, it reminds us of God's never-ending love. We might see Jesus, the good shepherd, in a stained glass window, or a carving of a vine with grapes on the altar, reminding us that Jesus is the true vine, or the cross in the front of the church, reminding us of Jesus' death and resurrection. Inside a church, even our sense of smell, in the lingering scent of incense, can remind us of God. All these scents and symbols call us to respond to God with love and thanksgiving.

Activity: God is depicted by a number of symbols and images in our liturgy. Read through Eucharistic Prayer A and write down as many images and symbols used to represent God as you find.

Throughout the liturgy our senses are stimulated. We see the cross and candles being carried to the altar, we listen to the word of God, we proclaim God's praises, we exchange the peace with our hands, we smell the scent of incense, and we eat and drink at the table. Using all our senses reminds us that Christ is alive with us today, guiding us and nourishing us. The richness of our worship is our response to the first commandment: To love God with all our heart, with all our soul, with all our mind, and with all our strength.

These sights, sounds, and smells are symbols of our faith. Each symbol is rich with meaning and experience. To understand the power of a symbol, think about the cross. It symbolizes the suffering of dying on the cross and the joy of the resurrection. For some people, it represents comfort in times of trouble, and for others, it represents the way Jesus conquered death. The cross carries all these meanings.

Parents and Mentors

Next time you are in church together, look carefully at the stained glass windows, the carvings on the altar, and the dressing on the altar. What symbols do you find? What do they represent?

Vestments

In the Episcopal Church, leaders of the liturgy usually wear vestments. **Vestments**, special garments set apart to be used only for worship, can make the Eucharist seem more reverent, and more like a celebration. Vestments are symbols, too. The stole is a long strip of cloth worn by a priest or bishop over both shoulders, or by a deacon over one shoulder and to the side. The Book of Common Prayer does not require particular vestments, but allows communities to follow their own customs. If you visit different churches throughout the year, you'll see a variety of colors and customs, and if you attend the National Acolyte Festival held each October at the National Cathedral in Washington, D.C., you'll see an amazing display of vestments and accessories. But some customs, such as the stole, are shared by all Episcopalians. The following list describes a number of vestments.

A **stole** is a strip of cloth worn by bishops and priests over both shoulders and by a deacon over the left shoulder.

An **alb** is a white garment worn by bishops, priests, deacons, and acolytes during the entire liturgy.

A **chasuble** is a long, sleeveless garment worn over the alb during the Liturgy of the Table. When laid out flat, it's generally oval with a hole in the middle for the celebrant's head. Chasubles vary in color based on the church season.

A **miter** is a tall pointed hat worn by the bishop.

A **crosier** is a pastoral staff that symbolizes the pastoral ministry of the bishop. A bishop generally holds the crosier during the reading of the Gospel, while walking in and out of the service, and during the absolution and blessing. It is a sign of authority.

The Church Year

Then God said, "Let there be Light"; and there was light. And God saw that the light was good; and God separated the light from the darkness. God called the light Day, and the darkness he called Night." (Genesis 1:3–5)

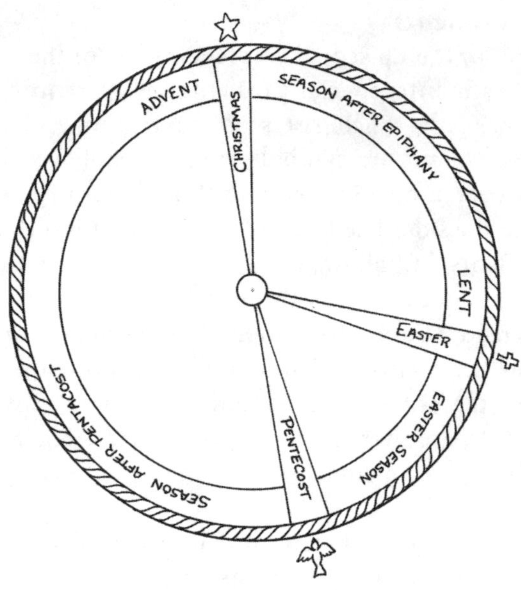

Calendar Wheel

Just like other communities, the church keeps track of time and seasons with a calendar. The church year gives us the chance to observe important events in Jesus' life and the life of the church. A common way to show the church year is with a calendar wheel as shown on the right. The calendar is anchored by two feasts—Christmas Day and Easter—which determine the dates of the seven seasons of the church year. Christmas is always December 25, while Easter Day is the first Sunday after the first full moon after the vernal equinox, March 21. The year begins with Advent, and going clockwise around the wheel, you can see that it continues with Christmas, the Season after Epiphany, Lent, Easter, Pentecost, and the Season after Pentecost. Each season is associated with a color that we use in church vestments, altar cloths, and banners. These colors remind us of each season.

The church year begins with Advent.

Activity: On page 880 of the Book of Common Prayer is a table for finding the date of Easter Day. On what date is the next Easter Day?

Advent. We begin the church year with **Advent** as we wait in expectation of Jesus' coming into the world—and his return at the end of time. Advent, which means "coming," begins four Sundays before Christmas Day. The color for Advent is either blue for hope of the peace that Christ brings or purple for penitence, or our request for forgiveness, as we prepare to welcome God's arrival as the Christ child.

Christmas. The season of **Christmas** begins on Christmas Day and ends twelve days later on January 6, the Feast of Epiphany. During Christmas we recall the stories of Christ's birth. Because Christmas is a time of celebration, its color is either white for purity or gold for royalty.

Epiphany. **Epiphany** means "to show forth." On the Feast of Epiphany—January 6—we celebrate the visit of the Magi to the Christ Child. On the first Sunday after the Feast of Epiphany we celebrate the baptism of Christ. The color of the Feast of Epiphany is white, while the rest of this season is green, which symbolizes life and growth. Epiphany ends on Ash Wednesday, the first day of Lent.

The colors of the church year seasons are:
- Advent—blue or purple
- Christmas—white or gold
- Season after Epiphany—green
- Lent—purple or linen
- Easter—white
- Pentecost—red
- Season after Pentecost—green

Lent. **Lent** is a time of prayer, fasting, and penitence in preparation for Easter. The early church used this time to train new believers in the faith, preparing them for baptism at the Great Vigil of Easter. The Great Vigil of Easter today is still a time for baptism. During Lent we renew our commitment to Christ and resolve to take on the difficult task of living as Christians in this world. Lent lasts forty days, beginning on Ash Wednesday and ending with the Saturday of Holy Week. If you count the days between Ash Wednesday and Holy Saturday, you'll find that there are forty-six days. From forty-six subtract the five Sundays during Lent and another one for Palm Sunday. We don't count these Sundays as part of Lent because Sundays celebrate Christ's resurrection. The color of Lent is purple for royalty and penitence, or rough linen, the color of sackcloth worn as a sign of mourning in stories of the Hebrew Scriptures. The color for the week between Palm Sunday and Easter is red for the death of Jesus.

Activity: Why is it especially appropriate to use the Great Litany during Lent? Why do you think that is so?

Three days in Holy Week, called the **Paschal Triduum** (Latin for "three days of Easter"), are the most sacred days of the church year. The Paschal Triduum begins with the Maundy Thursday service in the evening, peaks with the Great Vigil of Easter, and ends with the celebration of the Eucharist on Easter morning. On Maundy Thursday we remember three actions of Jesus: his washing the feet of the disciples, instituting, or starting, the sacrament of the Eucharist, and giving the new commandment:

"To love one another as I have loved you." This service comes right before the darkest day of the year—Good Friday, the day we remember Jesus' death on the cross.

Did You Know?

The word "Maundy" comes from the Latin word *mandatum* meaning "command." During the Last Supper, the meal commemorated on Maundy Thursday, Jesus gave a new commandment to his disciples that they should love one another.

Easter. The Great Vigil of Easter begins after sundown on Holy Saturday and ends before sunrise on Easter Sunday. It's the first service of Easter Day. During this service we light the Paschal candle to represent the light of the living Christ in our world, listen to the story of God's saving deeds in history, baptize new members, as well as celebrate Eucharist. The Great Vigil of Easter begins in the darkness of death and ends in the light of resurrected life.

Easter is so important that we celebrate it for not just one day but fifty days, beginning on Easter Sunday and ending with Pentecost Sunday. As a season of triumph, the color of Easter is white for purity. The fortieth day of Easter is Ascension Day, the day Jesus rose up into heaven. The final day of Easter is the Feast of Pentecost. On this day we celebrate the day the Holy Spirit came from heaven as tongues of fire and rested on the twelve apostles—this was the very beginning of the church. The color of the Feast of **Pentecost** is red, representing the fire of the Holy Spirit. In some churches the entire congregation is encouraged to wear red as a reminder that the Holy Spirit is among the people.

The word "Easter" comes from the Anglo-Saxon spring festival called Eostre. Easter replaced the pagan festival of Eostre.

Season after Pentecost. The days after Pentecost and before Advent are called the **Season after Pentecost**. It is the longest season of the church year, lasting anywhere from twenty-two to twenty-seven Sundays. This is a time for growing our faith and doing the work of ministry, emphasized by its liturgical color, green.

WORSHIP IS HOW WE GIVE THANKS TO GOD

Worship reflects a long and rich tradition that goes all the way back to when God first created the world. It our response to the many blessings that God gave us in creation and in Jesus, and continues to give us today.

Worship is how we give thanks to God. By intentionally participating in worship with our church families throughout the year, we will deepen our understanding of Jesus and God and our knowledge of God's desires for us. Joining a community in worship will prepare us for the work that God has given us to do.

Chapter 6

The Sacraments: Signs of Grace

The earth was cracked and dry. It hadn't rained for a long time. What should have been stalks of corn in the July fields were struggling, lanky sprouts, with little roots that could hardly break through the parched soil. But one day, clouds gathered and darkened the sky. The temperature dropped and the clouds broke open, squeezing the moisture out of the sky in torrents of rain and quenching the earth's thirst. The water loosened the soil, creating the space the roots needed to grow. The plants drank their fill. And when the rains stopped, the light of the sun spread its spectrum of colors across the sky in a glorious rainbow. The rainbow spread from horizon to horizon in a banner of every possible color—reds, oranges, yellows, greens, blues, indigos, and violets.

Most of us have seen a rainbow at one time or another. Each time one appears, it catches us by surprise and takes our breath. Seeing a rainbow fills our hearts with hope and joy. Why? One reason may be that we can't *make* a rainbow appear. It just appears as a part of creation. It's a free gift that represents new life and promise.

The ancient Israelites responded to rainbows in pretty much the same way we do. Remember the Bible story of Noah and the flood? God saw that the earth was corrupt and decided to destroy everything except for one righteous man named Noah, his family, and two of every kind of animal. Once they were all safe inside an ark, God sent fountains of rain for forty days and forty nights. All other people and animals were blotted out from the earth. After the flood, God made a covenant, or promise, with Noah, his descendents, and every living creature never to send a flood to destroy the earth again. God set a rainbow between heaven and earth as a sign of that covenant. That rainbow showed Noah and his family something they believed in their hearts—the promise of life and hope. Even today, the rainbow is a visible sign of a reality we can't see with our eyes but believe in our hearts—that God will always be with his people and all creation.

We are physical and spiritual beings. What we taste, touch, smell, hear, and see reveals that God dwells with us. Physical signs like the rainbow remind us of the power of unseen things. We can also experience God in music, sunrises, the scent of freshly baked bread, and the taste of wine.

Consider the power of an embrace. Can you remember a time when you had a fight with a friend or a brother or sister? Chances are, you got really angry and said some hurtful things. But after the fight was over and some time passed, you probably had second thoughts, and realized your mistakes. Oh, how good it feels to say "sorry," to extend a welcoming hand, or to share an embrace. You can almost feel that embrace, an outward sign, softening your heart, making room for forgiveness and reconciliation. That embrace is an outward and visible sign that represents an inward transformation.

That's exactly what a sacrament is—an outward sign of God's invisible, amazing grace. A rainbow and an embrace are outward signs of things we cannot see. The greatest outward sign God gave us of his love was Jesus. God came into the world in the person of Jesus, who was born at a particular time in a particular place. Jesus suffered for us on the cross. And God continues to be present in our lives through sacraments.

THE SACRAMENTS

Sacraments are "outward and visible signs of inward and spiritual grace, given by Christ as sure and certain means by which we receive that grace" (Book of Common Prayer, 857). The Episcopal Church recognizes two great sacraments of the Bible—baptism and Eucharist—and five sacramental rites—confirmation, ordination, holy matrimony, reconciliation of the penitent, and anointing of the sick. In Christ, God came to dwell among us. Through the Holy Spirit, God continues to dwell with us. In the sacraments we recognize God's active presence in our lives.

Each sacrament has a sign we can experience with our senses. We see, hear, and feel the water poured at baptism, we feel the hands of the bishop on us at confirmation, we see and feel on our hands the rings exchanged at marriage, we taste and smell the bread and wine for the Eucharist, and feel and smell the oil at the anointing of the sick. We can see, touch, smell, taste, and hear them.

Outward Visible Sign

The signs and gestures of the sacraments are living symbols that God the Father, God the Son, and God the Holy Spirit are alive in our human experiences. For each sacrament, an outward sign symbolizes the way grace transforms our hearts. The water of baptism, for example, is a symbol of dying and rebirth; eating and drinking the bread and wine of communion symbolizes refreshment and spiritual nourishment; the laying on of hands signifies the power of the Holy Spirit; wedding rings symbolize union; and the oil of anointing of the sick is a symbol of strengthening or healing. Through the sacraments Jesus enters our lives and continues the work of bringing us closer to God. God is with us here and now in very real and tangible ways. The table that follows summarizes the outward and visible signs and the inward and spiritual graces associated with each sacrament.

	Outward Visible Sign	**Inward Spiritual Grace**
Baptism	water	death to sin birth into God's family
Eucharist	bread and wine	body and blood of Christ forgiveness of sins strengthening of our union with Christ and one another foretaste of the heavenly banquet
Confirmation	laying on of hands by a bishop	strengthening of the Holy Spirit
Marriage	ring	union between a man and a woman
Reconciliation of a penitent	absolution by a priest	forgiveness of sins strength for right living

	Outward Visible Sign	Inward Spiritual Grace
Anointing of the sick	oil and/or laying on of hands	healing of mind, body, and spirit
Ordination	laying on of hands by a bishop for a priest and deacon and by three bishops for consecration of a bishop	authority and grace of the Holy Spirit

Inward Spiritual Grace

The power of the sacraments comes from God. Grace after all isn't something we can earn or achieve—God gives it to us freely and abundantly. And the effect of grace has nothing to do with the personal faith or moral character of the person presiding at a sacrament or the faith of the person receiving it, but with the power of the Holy Spirit.

We Respond

The rainbow is a sign of God's sacred covenant—an agreement that forms a relationship between God and creation. Throughout the Hebrew Scriptures, God reminds us, "You will be my people, and I will be your God." God will provide for his people, but his care requires us to respond—which our gift of free choice allows us to do.

We can respond by turning our hearts and minds to receive God's grace in each sacrament we receive. Baptism requires that we turn away from evil and accept Jesus Christ. Eucharist requires that we examine our lives, confess our sins, and be in good relationships with others. God showers grace on everyone, but like the seed that falls on rocky ground or fertile soil, we can either let the seed die or nurture it so that it bears fruit. So, let's look at each of the sacraments and explore the outward signs, inward graces, and what we can do to make the seed that is planted by grace grow strong in us.

BAPTISM

Do you not know that all of us who have been baptized into Christ Jesus were baptized into his death? Therefore we have been buried with him by baptism into death, so that, just as Christ was raised from the dead by the glory of the Father, so we too might walk in newness of life. (Romans 6:3–4)

We baptize in the Name of the Father, Son, and Holy Spirit. **Baptism** is full initiation by water and the Spirit into the body of Christ—the church. Through baptism God adopts us into his family. A necessary sacrament for all Christians, it's the foundation for all participation and ministry in the church.

The seashell is the symbol of baptism and is frequently found on baptismal fonts, the basin that holds the water for baptism.

Outward and Visible Sign

The water of baptism is rich with history and symbolism. God breathed over the waters at creation. God led the Israelites through the Red Sea into the Promised Land. In water, Jesus was baptized by John and anointed by the Holy Spirit. The water with which we baptize is this very same water of creation, freedom, and rebirth.

Activity: Read Mark 1:9–11. What were the visible signs at Jesus' baptism?

Inward and Spiritual Grace

By our baptism we share in the experiences of the creation, the freedom of the Israelites, and the baptism of Jesus. Through our baptism we also share in the death and resurrection of Jesus Christ. As Paul told the Romans in the passage that begins this section, at baptism our old selves die. Our sins are washed away. We are buried with Christ in his death and we share in his resurrection. Just as we burst into this world through the waters of our mother's womb, we come out of the waters of baptism as a new creation, reborn into God's family and marked as Christ's own forever. Through baptism, we all share, like ancient Israel, the promise of God's kingdom. In baptism we are brought into the community of believers. At baptism we receive God's grace in four ways: we become united with Christ, we're born into God's family, our sins are forgiven, and we receive new life in the Holy Spirit. Baptism is full initiation into the body of Christ. Nothing can take our membership away. In baptism we're sealed by the Holy Spirit and marked as Christ's own forever.

What's Required

In the early church, adults preparing for baptism, called **catechumens**, studied for two or three years before being baptized. Catechumens were allowed to attend Christian services, but only the Liturgy of the Word. The unbaptized had to leave before the Eucharist. Only when their lives conformed to the teachings of Christ and their faith was strong were they baptized and welcomed to participate in the holy mysteries of the Eucharist. Being a Christian in the early centuries, when the world was hostile toward the church, is much different than today. Years of preparation gave fledgling Christians the knowledge and strength needed to persevere in their new faith.

The inward and spiritual grace of baptism is:

- union with Christ
- birth into God's family
- forgiveness of sins
- new life in the Holy Spirit

Today, the Episcopal Church still requires candidates for baptism to take certain actions and make certain promises. They must turn *away* from evil (renounce Satan) and then turn *toward* Jesus Christ (accept Jesus as their Savior). In ancient liturgies, candidates faced the west to renounce Satan, then turned around toward the east to proclaim their faith in God. Today, in the service of Holy Baptism, candidates recall this early practice by three times renouncing Satan and three times accepting Jesus into their lives. When babies are baptized, the parents and godparents make these statements on the children's behalf. During the service of baptism, the congregation promises to support the newly baptized in their life in Christ.

Catechumens are people who are learning about God and the Christian faith. At the end of their study they may then become candidates for baptism.

Baptism transforms not just the one being baptized, but the whole body of Christ—every single member of the church. If you have younger siblings, you may remember how welcoming a new member into your family changed everyone's lives. It's the same when we welcome a new person into God's family. Together with the candidate, the community renews the Baptismal Covenant—professing a faith in God the Father; Jesus Christ, the Son of God; and God the Holy Spirit, and promising to continue to live a life in Christ.

EUCHARIST

> *When the hour came, he took his place at the table, and the apostles with him. He said to them, 'I have eagerly desired to eat this Passover with you before I suffer; for I tell you, I will not eat it until it is fulfilled in the kingdom of God.' Then he took a cup, and after giving thanks he said, 'Take this and divide it among yourselves; for I tell you that from now on I will not drink of the fruit of the vine until the kingdom of God comes.' Then he took a loaf of bread, and when he had given thanks, he broke it and gave it to them, saying, 'This is my body, which is given for you. Do this in remembrance of me.' And he did the same with the cup after supper, saying, 'This cup that is poured out for you is the new covenant in my blood.'* (Luke 22:14–20)

In the Episcopal Church we believe that by sharing the bread and the wine at communion we are made one with Christ. This is a belief of the Real Presence.

During the Last Supper, Jesus instituted, or started, the sacrament of Holy Eucharist with these words: "Do this in remembrance of me." Jesus took the bread and the wine, blessed it, offered thanks to God, and shared the meal with his friends. He instructed us to do the same. The bread and the wine are the outward and visible signs of the inward and spiritual grace of the body and blood of Christ.

According to belief within the Episcopal Church, Christ's body and blood are truly present in the consecrated bread and wine. This doctrine is called **Real Presence**. According to this belief, knowing *how* Christ is present in the sacraments is not central. What is central is the belief that by eating the bread and drinking the wine, recipients are united in communion with Christ. This doctrine contrasts with **transubstantiation**, the Roman Catholic and the Orthodox belief that when consecrated, the substance of the bread and the wine are transformed into the substance of Christ's body and blood, while the appearance as bread and wine continues to be unchanged. The Episcopal Church instead embraces the belief of Real Presence.

Activity: Look up the words to Hymn 322 in the 1982 Hymnal. What doctrine does this hymn reflect—transubstantiation or Real Presence? Explain your answer.

The Purpose of Holy Eucharist

Through the celebration of Holy Eucharist we remember Jesus' life, death, and resurrection, and await his coming again in glory. We understand the celebration of Eucharist as a **memorial**, not as a re-enactment of a past event of the Last Supper. As Episcopalians, we see Holy Eucharist as declaring that Christ is among us, a living sacrifice, for us today. The Eucharist makes God's saving acts we read about in the Bible and our expectation of Jesus' return a part of us today.

A way to understand what we mean by memorial is to learn the word anamnesis. **Anamnesis** is an active form of memory that connects the past to the present in a way that allows us to become a present participant in the past event. Have you ever smelled perfume that reminded you of someone so much that you could almost hear her voice or the pattern of her footsteps nearby? You look around, feeling her presence as if she were with you. That is anamnesis—a remembrance of a past event in a way that it becomes present to you today.

The inward and spiritual grace of Eucharist is

- forgiveness of sins
- strengthening of our union with Christ and one another
- foretaste of the heavenly banquet

In the Eucharist, the past events that become present to you are God's saving actions throughout history—at creation, in the covenant made with Israel, and most of all in the life, death, and resurrection of Jesus. Not only are past events made present to us, so are the future events of the heavenly banquet—when we'll become fully one with God.

Another word—*kairos*—might help. You and I are most familiar with a linear progression of time with a distinct past, present, and future—think of the timelines you might find in your history textbook, for example. This type of clock time is called *chronos*. But there's another way of thinking about time. **Kairos** transcends time and instead defines the *quality* of a particular moment. In kairos, all time collapses into one moment. In the kairos of the Eucharist, we can partake in all of God's saving acts—past, present and future—when God draws us close to him. Through Eucharist we're forgiven our past sins, strengthened in our current union with Christ,

Anamnesis is when you remember something so strongly it's as if it is happening today.

Time at Eucharist is not like the time we experience when the clock ticks. It is the collapse of all times–past, present and future–into one moment. This kind of time is kairos.

and given a taste of heaven. Jesus often talked about heaven as an elaborately prepared meal. An image that we commonly use to refer to heaven therefore is a banquet. In kairos, time collapses into one moment, in the Eucharist—a concentrated dose of communion with God and all of creation.

What's Required

Holy Eucharist is a necessary part of living a life in Christ. Because by our nature we're separated from God, we continually do things that aren't good for us, for others, or for creation and we need forgiveness and healing. Through Holy Communion we're forgiven and our relationship with Christ is strengthened. We come before Christ willingly and longing to be in a good relationship with all people. So before Eucharist we examine our lives to see where we've fallen short, confess our sins, and make amends with those we have hurt.

The Liturgy of the Word prepares us for better relationships with God and other people. On most Sundays, the entire congregation says the confession together, admitting our shortcomings and asking God for mercy. After the priest pronounces God's forgiveness with absolution, we exchange the peace. Exchanging the peace is a sign that we have forgiven one another for anything we've done to hurt others. After the peace, we're ready for Holy Communion.

Absolution is the act of pronouncing that God has forgiven our sins.

CONFIRMATION

When he came to Nazareth, where he had been brought up, he went to the synagogue on the sabbath day, as was his custom. He stood up to read, and the scroll of the prophet Isaiah was given to him. He unrolled the scroll and found the place where it was written:

'The Spirit of the Lord is upon me,
because he has anointed me to bring good news to the poor.
He has sent me to proclaim release to the captives
and recovery of sight to the blind, to let the oppressed go free,
to proclaim the year of the Lord's favor.'

And he rolled up the scroll, gave it back to the attendant, and sat down. The eyes of all in the synagogue were fixed on him. Then he

> *began to say to them, 'Today this scripture has been fulfilled in your hearing.' All spoke well of him and were amazed at the gracious words that came from his mouth. They said, 'Is not this Joseph's son?'* (Luke 4:16–22)

In this passage, Jesus announces to his hometown that he's been called to serve. In the eyes of his fellow villages, Jesus had grown from a baby presented to God in the Temple to a young man reading in the synagogue, proclaiming his purpose as God's son. The elders, looking at Joseph's son, are amazed and probably a bit surprised as they watched him announce the ministry God has given him to do.

At baptism we're reborn, like infants, to a new family of God. As we continue in life, like Jesus, we grow within the community. Through experience and learning we gain knowledge of Christ, ourselves, God's call for us, and our community. Through practice, we exercise and strengthen our gifts for ministry.

At some point as we mature into adulthood, we're expected to affirm the faith that others proclaimed for us at baptism, and to renew our baptismal promises as God's call to us. Confirmation is the rite in which we do this. **Confirmation** is the rite in which we make a mature commitment to Christ and receive continuing strength from the Holy Spirit. During the rite of confirmation, we reaffirm our rejection of evil and renew our commitment to Jesus Christ. And just as they did at our baptism, the congregation promises to do all in their power to support us in our life in Christ. Then together the candidates and the congregation renew the Baptismal Covenant.

Activity: Read the first part of the Rite of Confirmation on page 415 of the Book of Common Prayer. What gives the candidates for confirmation the ability to follow Christ as their Savior and Lord?

Outward and Visible Sign and Inward and Spiritual Grace

After the candidates renew their Baptismal Covenants, the bishop lays hands on them, asking God to strengthen and empower them for service. This follows the example of Jesus, who throughout his ministry laid his hands on those whom he healed and blessed. This physical contact powerfully shows how power is given to the one being blessed. The bishop also prays, asking God to give the candidates the strength of the Holy Spirit, to nourish them for continued life in Christ.

The laying on of hands and the prayer are the outward and visible signs of confirmation. The laying on of hands is a sign expressing God's power given to the confirmand. The inward and spiritual grace of confirmation is a renewal and strengthening of the Holy Spirit in the life of the candidate.

The outward sign of confirmation is laying on of hands; the inward grace is strengthening by the Holy Spirit.

What's Required of the Candidate

Candidates for confirmation must be baptized. Because confirmation is a mature commitment to a life in Christ, candidates must also know about Christian faith—what Christians believe and what it means to follow Christ. Candidates must also confess their sins and be ready to say that Jesus Christ is their Lord and Savior.

Remember that those who are baptized are already full members of the body of Christ. Confirmation doesn't complete their initiation, nor is it necessary to be confirmed before receiving communion. Confirmation is an opportunity for those who are baptized to make a mature and independent affirmation of their faith.

MARRIAGE

> *For you were called to freedom, brothers and sisters; only do not use your freedom as an opportunity for self-indulgence, but through love become slaves to one another. For the whole law is summed up in a single commandment, "You shall love your neighbor as yourself."*
> (Galatians 5:13–14)

The outward sign of marriage is a ring; the inward grace is the union of two people.

All people are called to faithful relationships with others. Some are called to Holy Matrimony. **Holy Matrimony** is the physical and spiritual binding together of two people before God and his people for mutual joy, with the intention of a lifelong commitment. After making their vows to one another, the couple exchange rings as signs of the vows by which they bind themselves to each other. The rings are the outward sign of the inward grace of union.

A Covenant Relationship

Marriage is a covenant, a binding agreement that is freely entered by two people. In marriage, two people bind themselves to one another in the presence of God. As a covenant, marriage mirrors God's relationship with his chosen people and Christ's relationship to the church.

We've already learned that our relationship with God is a covenant relationship. God initiated a covenant with the Hebrews, promising to be their God and to make them his people, and requiring them to "be faithful; to love justice, do mercy, and walk humbly with their God" (Book of Common Prayer, 847). God renewed the covenant through Christ, granting us salvation and requiring that we believe in Jesus and keep his commandments. In both covenants, God makes promises and the people are required, but not forced, to respond. The covenant requires a response, an action by all those entering it. The same is true with the covenant of marriage. The couple freely make promises to one another.

What's Required

Those who marry come to know the Scripture passage that opens this section deeply. Each person in a marriage freely serves the other and honors the central commandment to love your neighbor as yourself. They've promised to love, comfort, honor, and keep, and, forsaking all others, be faithful to each other. They've promised to love and serve each other in all circumstances of life. Every couple faces tough situations sometime during their marriage, but even though they may argue, they've promised to love one another anyway. If one of them becomes ill, the other has promised to care for the other in his or her need. And if one of them meets somebody they think they like better, they remember that they've promised to forsake all others.

Activity: Read "Concerning the Service" on page 422 of the Book of Common Prayer. What are the three requirements for the Celebration and Blessing of a Marriage?

God has bound the couple together and has given them his abundant grace and power to keep their promises. During the marriage ceremony, the priest asks for God's blessing and assistance to keep their promises of faithfulness and love. In a public ceremony, the Christian community also promises to uphold the couple in their marriage.

Procreation and Sexual Intimacy

Marriage is a gift from God for mutual joy and companionship. It exists so that two people can express their mutual love, their love can be sustained by God, and the community, and the two can share their love with others.

When it's God's will, marriage is also for having and raising children. We add "when it's God's will" because not all couples bear or raise children. The sacrament of marriage grants grace to a couple and to a community, whether they have children or not.

Sexual intimacy is part of God's creation. Through sexual intercourse we create new life and participate in God's creative acts. Sexual intercourse strengthens the union of the couple, drawing them into communion of body and soul, further binding the two into mutual companionship and strengthening their life together. Sexual intimacy is one way a married couple expresses their deep and abiding love for each other. The depth of intimacy shared between two people leaves a lasting mark of each person's body and soul on the other.

RECONCILIATION OF A PENITENT

> *Jesus said to them again, "Peace be with you. As the Father has sent me, so I send you." When he had said this, he breathed on them and said to them, "Receive the Holy Spirit. If you forgive the sins of any, they are forgiven them; if you retain the sins of any, they are retained."* (John 20:21–23)

The first words that the risen Christ said to the disciples were, "Peace be with you." Jesus would have used the Hebrew word for peace, "shalom," which has a much broader meaning of wholeness, health, prosperity, and right relationships. This was Christ's gift to the world. Right after giving them his peace, Jesus tells his disciples to forgive sins in his name. Forgiveness is central to our life as Christians and to shalom.

We practice confession and receive forgiveness regularly in our worship together. Together we confess that we haven't loved God with our whole heart and haven't loved our neighbor as ourselves. We confess that we have fallen short of God's desires for us and ask for forgiveness, and the priest expresses God's forgiveness of us. As a people reconciled to one another, we then share the peace—the same peace that Christ offered the disciples.

We may also confess our sins in the sacrament of reconciliation. **Reconciliation of a Penitent** is "the rite in which those who repent of their sins may confess them to God in the presence of a priest, and receive the assurance of pardon and the grace of absolution" (Book of Common Prayer, 861). The outward and visible sign of reconciliation is the laying on of hands. The inward and spiritual grace is restoration of a right relationship with God and the body of Christ.

Sin

To understand the need for repentance and reconciliation, let's look at what sin is. Because we're separated from God, it's our nature to sin. We don't always listen to the will of God because our own desires and egos get in the way. The Hebrew word for sin is *het*, which translated literally means "miss the mark." When we sin we miss the mark of what God wants for us.

The Catechism defines sin as "seeking our own will instead of the will of God, thus distorting our relationship with God, with other people, and with all creation" (Book of Common Prayer, 848). The Ten Commandments explicitly state our duty to God and our neighbors. Actions contrary to these commandments distort our relationship with God and others.

Jesus gave us the two commandments that form the foundation of all of God's laws: "You shall love the Lord your God with all your heart, and with all your soul, and with all your mind" and "You shall love your neighbor as yourself." These two commandments provide the basis for examining our lives and understanding when we've sinned. When have you not loved God? When have you not loved yourself? When have you not loved your neighbor?

Repenting: Changing Direction

God longs for our pardon and peace. God sent Jesus to bear our sins on the cross and to reconcile us to God. And the risen Christ proclaimed God's desire to the disciples with his greeting of "peace." We're called to repent as a regular part of our worship together. Morning Prayer, Evening Prayer, and Holy Eucharist all include the call to repent, an opportunity for a general confession, and a general absolution. God continually offers his healing grace and pardon. Our response is to examine our lives, repent of our sins, and firmly resolve to do better.

> The word "repentance" comes from the Greek word that means to change direction. When we repent we turn *away* from sin by confessing what we have done wrong and turn *toward* God by promising to do what is right.

The sacrament of reconciliation helps us change our hearts and live according to God's will. It's not a necessary service, but everyone can take part in it if they want to. For some people, a general absolution isn't enough—they may need help and advice to make amends. They may have committed a serious offense for which they doubt they may be pardoned. They may need the strength of the church to face their sins. The sacrament of reconciliation provides the benefit of absolution, the assurance of forgiveness, spiritual counsel and advice, and the strengthening of faith.

What's Required

God always offers us abundant, forgiving grace. Pardon isn't something we deserve. It's freely given. We respond to this grace by recognizing the need to change. It's God's grace that is the source of our repentance. We prepare for the rite of reconciliation by:

1. Examining our actions and inactions for unfaithfulness.
2. Expressing our regret and sorrow.
3. Setting our resolve to conform to God's will.

In each of these, we acknowledge our complete reliance on the grace of God alone. We need to acknowledge to God where we've missed the mark. It's through God's yearning for wholeness that we feel regret and sorrow. And it's with God's strength that we work to conform to God's will.

Parents and Mentors

Read the Parable of the Lost Coin together (Luke 15:8–10). What three things does the woman do once she realizes that she has lost the coin? What does she do when she finds the coin? How did God feel?

The Rite of Reconciliation

The rite of reconciliation can take place anywhere—after all, as Jesus promised us, he is present wherever two people meet in his name. But, generally, the penitent and the priest meet face-to-face in the priest's office or study, or in the church.

The penitent begins by asking for a blessing. That shows that we need God's help to examine ourselves and confess our sins. The penitent continues by confessing to God and the church his or her offenses, expressing a resolve to amend sinful ways, and asking for God's forgiveness. The priest serves as a witness to the confession. After the confession, the priest responds by offering counsel and advice. The priest then lays hands on the penitent and pronounces God's forgiveness. The penitent thanks God. The priest concludes by saying, "Go in peace, and pray for me, a sinner." This final request reminds us that the penitent and the priest stand together in need of God's mercy.

A penitent is someone who is sorry for his or her sins and is seeking reconciliation.

Activity: Read "Concerning the Rite" on page 446 of the Book of Common Prayer. If a layperson or deacon hears a confession, how will the service be different than if a priest hears it?

Role of the Priest

We confess to and receive absolution by a priest for many reasons. Priests have the gifts of wisdom and counsel necessary to give good advice. But more importantly, we can be pardoned only by those whom we have offended. Since sins are an offense to God, only God can forgive. God gave Jesus the authority to forgive sins and Jesus gave that authority to the apostles. This authority is also given to priests. They, therefore, have the authority to proclaim God's pardon on God's behalf. A second reason we confess to a priest is that any sin affects the entire community by weakening relationships and separating the sinner from the community. Because a priest represents the body of Christ, a priest also grants pardon on behalf of the community. Through reconciliation, our relationship with God, others, and creation is made right.

Confidentiality

Confession is always confidential. A priest can never reveal the contents of a confession to anyone. Civil law in the United States honors this confidentiality so that even in a court of law a priest cannot be made to tell what's been said in confession. This provides the penitent the security of complete silence. The sins revealed are held in God's loving embrace and the silence of the church.

HEALING OF THE SICK

> *Are any among you sick? They should call for the elders of the church and have them pray over them, anointing them with oil in the name of the Lord. The prayer of faith will save the sick, and the Lord will raise them up; and anyone who has committed sins will be forgiven.* (James 5:14–15)

This passage from James tells us that healing serves two purposes: to raise up the sick and to forgive their sins. **Unction of the Sick** is "the rite of anointing the sick with oil, or the laying on of hands, by which God's grace is given for the healing of spirit, mind, and body" (Book of Common Prayer, 861).

Outward and Visible Sign

The outward and visible sign of healing is anointing with oil and/or the laying on of hands. Oil has been used for healing since ancient times. The Good Samaritan cared for the man who'd been robbed by bandaging his wounds with oil and wine, showing the comfort of oil and the power of touch. The disciples anointed the sick with oil. Oil seeps into the pores of the skin, penetrating deep into the body. Jesus' healings highlight how important touch is to healing. Jesus rubbed spit into the eyes of a blind man and brought his sight back. A sick woman touched Jesus' robe and was healed. Jesus put his fingers into the ears of a deaf man and restored his hearing.

> The outward sign of healing is laying on of hands and anointing with oil. The inward grace is healing of body, mind, and spirit.

Inward and Spiritual Grace

Healing is a sacrament of faith that follows the example of the healing ministry of Jesus. Through healing, Jesus made life whole and proclaimed that God's kingdom would be restored.

Healing raises up the sick to God's healing power, which brings the strength, courage, and peace needed to face the realities of our broken world, including disease and mental and physical pain. Sickness weakens the spirit. Healing seeks to strengthen the spirit. Sickness isolates individuals, so healing restores the sick to community. Sickness brings despair. Healing seeks to renew hope.

Healing does not necessarily mean curing. When we look for a cure, we are seeking the end of an illness or disease. Being healed could mean that the disease is gone. We hear many stories of Jesus healing people miraculously—lepers were cured, the blind could see, and the lame could walk. But healing can also be receiving the strength to live with an illness or to grow spiritually as the result of living with disease. Healing can also be mending broken relationships. The laying on of hands and anointing with oil makes Christ and Christ's healing power present to us.

Healing can be done privately or publicly. Many churches offer healing as part of, or shortly after, the Sunday service. During the rite of healing, the priest lays hands on the person and prays to God for healing. If anointing is offered, the priest dips a thumb in the oil and makes the sign of the cross on the person's forehead, anointing in the name of the Father, the Son and the Holy Spirit.

Activity: Pastoral Offices are services that are done in response to pastoral need. In which Pastoral Office is the sacramental rite of healing?

ORDINATION

> *Then Jesus went about all the cities and villages, teaching in their synagogues, and proclaiming the good news of the kingdom, and curing every disease and every sickness. When he saw the crowds, he had compassion for them, because they were harassed and helpless, like sheep without a shepherd. Then he said to his disciples, 'The harvest is plentiful, but the laborers are few; therefore ask the Lord of the harvest to send out laborers into his harvest.'* (Matthew 9:35–38)

This passage from the Gospel according to Matthew offers a vision of church leadership dedicated to teaching, proclaiming the good news, and caring for the people. Faced with the crowds who were "like sheep without a shepherd," Jesus knows they need people to serve them. **Ordination** is a gift from God that provides men and women to care for God's people and to proclaim the gospel.

Three Holy Orders

All baptized Christians are called to represent Christ and act in ways that bring God's love to the world. God calls some Christians to the holy orders of bishop, priest, or deacon.

Ordained ministers are living reminders of the church's life and mission. Bishops are a symbol that the church is the one, catholic, and apostolic church, as we say in the Apostles' Creed. Bishops remind us that the people of God are one and that the church today is part of the church that was born with the apostles. Priests are a sign of the teaching of the gospel and the breaking of the bread celebrated by the church. Deacons are a sign that the church is a servant to the poor and others in the world who are in need. Bishops, priests, and deacons serve the church so that we—the laity—can serve as the body of Christ to the world.

The primary ministry of the **bishop** (and all ministers) is to "represent Christ and his Church." The ministry unique to a bishop is to oversee a diocese. The bishop fulfills this role as a diocese's primary teacher, pastor, and priest. As teacher, the bishop is responsible for making sure that the Christian faith is taught faithfully. As pastor, the bishop serves the pastoral needs of the priests in the diocese and their families. As priest, the bishop has the authority to ordain priests and deacons, to confirm the baptized, and to bless a church. Bishops also symbolize the unity of the church.

A diocese is the primary geographic and administrative unit of the Episcopal Church. All the churches in a diocese share the diocese's bishop or bishops.

They do so because they stand in a succession of bishops all the way back to the apostles who were sent out to make believers of all people. Bishops connect the church today to the first community of believers. Because bishops uphold the belief of the church as founded by the apostles, they also connect all the many individual churches into one Christian church.

A **priest** serves the church primarily as pastor to the people and shares the responsibility of overseeing the church with the bishop. In that role, priests celebrate Holy Eucharist and baptize. A priest also blesses people and grants absolution of sins in the name of God. Priests are also given the role of teaching and proclaiming the gospel, a ministry they share with all the baptized.

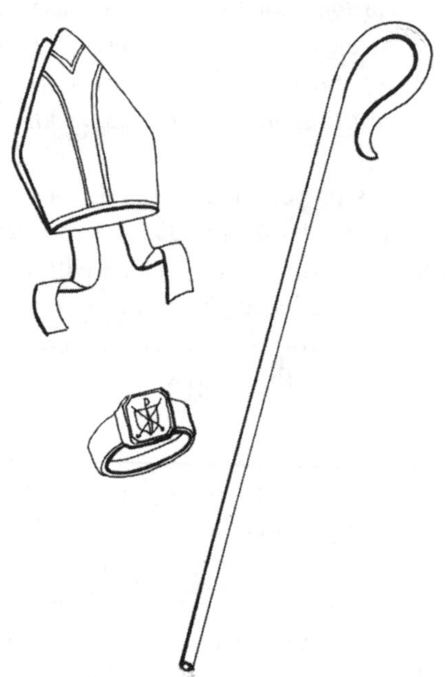

The bishop's staff is a symbol of pastoral authority. The bishop's ring is a sign of fidelity and bond to the church. The miter is a bishops's hat.

A **deacon** has a unique ministry of servanthood. Deacons are called to be outward signs of the servant ministry of the church to the poor, the sick, and the hungry. They represent Christ's ministry of healing to the world. Deacons are also called to support the ministry of all baptized members of the church out in the world. A person who wishes to be ordained a priest must first be ordained a deacon. Not all deacons, however, are called to be priests. The diaconate is a religious order in its own right.

The word "deacon" comes from the Greek word *diakonos,* meaning ministry or servant.

The Sacrament of Ordination

A person who is called by God and recognized by the church to the order of bishop, priest, or deacon is ordained by prayer and the laying on of hands by a bishop. A bishop is consecrated by the laying on of hands by three other bishops. The laying on of hands is the outward and visible sign of ordination. The inward and spiritual grace is the authority of the Holy Spirit, which helps bishops as they minister to the church.

Let's explore the service for the ordination of a priest. First, a priest and a lay person present the candidate to the bishop. That's because the call by God to ordination is identified by both the individual and the community. Preparing for ordination takes at least eighteen months and includes education about beliefs, practical experience, emotional development, and spiritual formation. At ordination, people who know and support the candidate state their belief that the candidate is qualified and suitable for the ordained ministry.

After the presentation, the candidate declares that the Holy Scriptures are the Word of God and contain all things necessary to salvation, and promises to conform to the doctrine, discipline, and worship of the church. Finally, the congregation expresses its desire that the candidate be ordained and promises to uphold him or her in the ministry. As with the other sacraments, ordination is celebrated in community, showing that we're one body in Christ.

Activity: What six promises does a candidate to the priesthood make? You can find the promises on page 532 of the Book of Common Prayer.

Before consecration, the bishop examines the candidate to determine whether his or her calling is true. The bishop also asks the candidate to promise to pursue the disciplines necessary to fulfill the ministry. The bishop ends the examination by asking God to grant the candidate the grace and power to fulfill those promises.

At the consecration, the bishop gives praise and thanksgiving to God for his love, his call to us, and his gift of Jesus. Together with the priests who are present, the bishop lays hands on the candidate and asks God to grant the power and grace of the Holy Spirit to make him or her a priest in the church.

The outward sign of ordination is laying on of hands. The inward grace is authority and grace of the Holy Spirit.

Once and Always a Bishop, Priest, or Deacon

Ordination means a lifelong ministry. Unless bishops, priests, or deacons renounce their vows, or are removed from their ministry by some serious offense—and whether or not they have paid positions in the church—they are ordained persons until death.

LIFE AS A SACRAMENT

As people of God we live sacramental lives, receiving God's grace every day through the many signs of his dwelling with us. God uses material things to reach out to us in unlimited ways. The embrace of a friend, a gentle smile, sharing a meal, the blessing of a mother to her child are just a few examples. Open your eyes to the world and God's actions in it. Look for the rainbows. Visible signs will keep you hopeful and give you the grace to live a holy life. Sacraments—outward signs of God's grace—are not just inside church buildings. They're everywhere you look. We can all draw closer to God by opening our eyes to them.

Chapter 7

Spirituality: Created for Prayer

When I was a young child, my father would tell me to take some time every day to be by myself. I really didn't know *what* I was supposed to do. I thought I was with myself all the time! In fact, so much so that sometimes I wanted to crawl out of my skin. Daytime was my time to be busy, spending time with my friends and being involved in lots of activities. But I usually gave in to my dad's strange suggestion and dragged my feet to the hammock in our backyard.

As I lay there in the gentle rocking of the hammock and stared up into the canopy of leaves above, I soon forgot that I was mad at my father for making me be alone. The voice of anger quieted and I'd begin to notice the quietness of the day and the warm rays of sun making their ways through the leaves. Soon, I noticed a voice inside of me and I listened. I listened to its goodness and love. I didn't recognize it at the time, but these were times of prayer, times when I was filled with God's love and presence. Today I yearn to recapture those long afternoons of listening.

If you stop to think about it, you may be surprised at how much you pray during the day. Do you think about what life is all about while doodling on the side of your school papers? Do you pray for those in need when you hear the ambulance siren? Do you say grace before a meal or a quick prayer before a test? Sometimes blaring music can be a way of clearing your mind of the noise of the world. Believe it or not, sometimes through the blaring music comes the still small voice of God. (It's also true that blaring music can be just noise to help you avoid that still small voice.)

A RELATIONSHIP WITH GOD

Parents and Mentors

Prayer can be sharing a meal. Read John 21:1–14 together. How do you think the disciples felt eating breakfast with Jesus?

Because we're created by God, it's only natural for us to yearn for a relationship with him. Our God loves us deeply and is constantly calling us closer. The Bible is filled with examples of people talking with God. God asked Noah to build an ark. Abraham negotiated with God to save the city of Sodom. Hannah asked God for a son. Moses spoke with God lots of times—revealing his own weaknesses and telling God, "I can't do it." Jesus was in constant conversation with God. In fact, we might say that Jesus lived a life of unceasing prayer.

Activity: Read the following passages: Matthew 4:1–2; 6:9–13; 11:1; 11:25–26; 14:19–21. What spiritual discipline did Jesus practice in each passage?

What does it mean that Jesus lived a life of unceasing prayer? Well, Jesus spent time alone and in silence, an activity many of us easily identify as prayer. One example is when Jesus went up the mountains by himself after feeding those five thousand people who had come to hear him preach (Matthew 14). But a life of unceasing prayer is more than just getting away from it all every now and then. It's acknowledging God's presence in all that we do. It's living our lives in a close relationship with God. Jesus spent much of his years of ministry among people, studying, fasting, celebrating, worshipping, and just enjoying their company. These are all *spiritual disciplines* that support a life of unceasing prayer. **Spiritual disciplines** are intentional practices—habits we form on purpose—that keep us in dialogue with God. Spiritual disciplines reinforce a life of unceasing prayer—and are also the result of unceasing prayer.

Prayer is experiencing the presence of God through words, actions, or silence.

Lots of spiritual disciplines can bring you to a closer relationship with God. We're not meant to practice all the disciplines all the time. Some are appropriate for particular seasons of the year. Lent, for example, is a season of fasting, while Easter is a season of celebration. Not every discipline suits everybody. It's like any other activity—you might love to go for long bike rides, while your best friend is happiest when she's swimming laps in the pool. Take a look at each of the spiritual practices that follow and decide which ones might help you find a closer relationship with God.

PRAYER

When we have conversations with friends, we generally don't talk about only one topic. Sometimes we share a hurt or a celebration. At other times we might say how much we appreciate their friendship or give them a compliment. If we've hurt a friend we might ask for forgiveness to restore our friendship. Our conversations with God are just as real and just as diverse.

Activity: How does the Catechism define prayer? What is Christian prayer? See page 856 in the Book of Common Prayer.

The principal kinds of prayer are adoration, confession, thanksgiving, intercession, and petition. A good way to remember them is the acronym ACTIP, one letter for each of the five fingers on your hand. Prayers of **adoration** are words and actions that express our love for God and creation. An example is the Gloria during Eucharist, when we sing or say, "Glory to God in the highest!" We ask for nothing; we just praise God.

In a prayer of **confession**, we admit that we've done something wrong, turn away from sin, and seek to restore our relationship with others through God. An example of a prayer of confession is the general confession during worship, in which we say, "We have not loved you with our whole heart. . . . We are truly sorry and we humbly repent."

When we express our gratitude to God for all the blessings and mercies we've received, we're offering a prayer of **thanksgiving**. After arriving home from a long-distance trip with my family I thank God for the time I spent with my husband and two children and for our safe return home.

There are five kinds of prayer—one for each finger of your hand. An easy way to remember is with the acronym ACTIP:

Adoration
Confession
Thanksgiving
Intercession
Petition

Intercessions are requests for God's blessings and healing grace for others. The Prayers of the People, when we pray for the church, our nation, our community, and people in trouble, are prayers of intercession. We are praying to God for other people.

Petitions are requests for God's blessings and grace for ourselves. We might ask God for guidance in making a decision, protection from evil, or the healing of pain.

We can pray in ways other than with words. Actions such as kneeling in confession or lifting up our hands in praise are prayer too. When you pray, you don't have to include a prayer of every type. Let your heart guide your prayer.

Activity: Identify words of adoration, confession, and petition in the Lord's Prayer.

THE DAILY OFFICE

The **Daily Office** in the Book of Common Prayer is a disciplined way of acknowledging God's presence in our lives through daily prayer and readings. With Morning Prayer, we declare the day sacred and invite God to begin the day with us. In the morning hours of new light we look forward to the day, praising God, maker of heaven and earth. As the sun sets, we turn to Evening Prayer to reflect on the day and thank God for providing a Savior, a light to enlighten the nations.

The word "office" comes from the Latin word meaning duty. Monks considered it their duty to pray for the whole world during set times of the day.

The Shema: "Hear, O Israel, the LORD is our God, the LORD alone. You shall love the LORD your God with all your heart, and with all your soul, and with all your might" (Deuteronomy 6:4).

Setting aside time each day for prayer and study gives us the opportunity to invite God into our daily routine, to recognize that God is always at work in our lives, and to respond to God's presence with praise and thanksgiving. The practice of praying daily dates back to the times of the Hebrew Scriptures. The Israelites said the *Shema*, a declaration of faith, two or three times a day. Psalm 119 says, "Seven times a day I praise you." Jesus and the disciples prayed daily and so did early Christian communities. Early Christian communities continued the Jewish practice of marking their days with prayer. In the early centuries of the church, some Christians organized and lived in **monastic communities**. A monastic community is a group of Christians who live away from society and dedicate themselves to simple lives of study, prayer, and service—ordered rules. Early communities developed seven daily offices—or times of prayer—beginning with Lauds (morning prayer) upon waking and ending with Compline before going to sleep. The hours of their prayers were:

Monastic communities are groups of religious people who choose to live in community and take vows to live in a specific way. Common vows are poverty, chastity, and obedience.

Matins and Lauds	daybreak
Prime, the first hour	6 am

Terce, the third hour	9 am
Sext, the sixth hour	noon
None, the ninth hour	3 pm
Vespers	sunset
Compline	bedtime

The Daily Offices in our prayer book are based on these monastic offices. Just as in the monastic offices, both Evening and Morning Prayer are made up of the Psalms, Scripture, and prayers. We call these elements the Invitatory and Psalter, the Lessons, and the Prayers. The **Invitatory** is a sentence and response that invites our hearts and minds to the purpose of the gathering. In Morning Prayer, for example, we say,

Officiant Lord, open our lips.
People And our mouth shall proclaim your praise.

And at Evening Prayer we begin with

Officiant O God, make speed to save us.
People O Lord, make haste to help us.

Notice the difference in the tone between Morning and Evening Prayer. At day's break we begin with praise and thank God for the day to come. After the day has passed, we ask for God's forgiveness, knowing that we've fallen short of what God calls us to do.

A psalm is known by its opening phrase in Latin. Psalm 121 is called *Levavi oculos* because its first phrase is "I lift up my eyes."

In the morning the Invitatory and Psalter continue with an antiphon, the *Venite* or *Jubilate*, and a psalm. **Antiphons** are sentences, usually from the Bible, that we say before and after the psalm. The *Venite* (Psalm 95:1–7) and the *Jublilate* (Psalm 100) invite us to rejoice in the God of creation and praise the goodness of our God. In the evening we say the *Phos Hilaron* ("O Gracious Light"), which acknowledges the ending of the day and the light that God brings into the world through Jesus Christ.

Activity: Look on page 112 of the Book of Common Prayer. What is the *Phos Hilaron*? In which Daily Office do we say the *Phos Hilaron*? Why do you think this is so?

Both offices continue with a psalm followed by one or more Lessons. You can find the cycle of psalms and readings for each day in the back pages of the Book of Common Prayer, beginning on page 934. If you follow the cycle of psalms and readings for the two-year cycle, you'll have read a lot of the Bible. After the lessons we say a **canticle**, a "little song" based on Scripture, and the Apostles' Creed. The traditional canticles for Evening Prayer are the *Magnificat*, the song of Mary in Luke's story of the birth of Jesus, and the *Nunc dimittis*, the song of Simeon when he saw the Christ Child, also in Luke's gospel. Both canticles acknowledge God's greatness and gift of salvation through Jesus Christ.

The final element of both offices is the Prayers, including the Lord's Prayer. With the prayers, we give thanks and ask God to remember our needs as well as the needs of our community, both close by and around the world.

Both Evening and Morning Prayer have optional begin with an opening sentence of Scripture, confession, and absolution. Evening Prayer can also begin with "The Service of Light" that focuses on the fading of the day and acknowledges that even the darkness is radiant in God's sight. Oremus.org publishes the Daily Office online.

The Book of Common Prayer offers two additional daily prayers: Noonday Prayer for midday and Compline, said just before turning into bed for the night. For those whose days don't have room for these liturgies, the prayer book provides shorter "Daily Devotions for Individuals." Whether you pray the offices alone or in a group, when you pray, you pray with a communion of believers throughout the world.

SILENCE AND LISTENING

Prayer is a conversation. It requires the presence of you and God. While God is always with us, we aren't always with God. Most of us aren't in tune with God's presence. We think prayer is telling God all about ourselves and often we allow little time for God to talk to us. Think of prayer as tuning to a radio station where you can hear God speaking. Most times we're tuned into other radio stations—ones where we are hearing our friends or our culture tell us what's important. So, you might think of praying as a way to tune out your friends and advertising, and scan the frequencies until you find God. The spiritual exercises that follow will help you find *your* channel, a channel to listen to what God has to say, and offer your own words now and then, too. The following are practices you might try to find God's voice.

Centering Prayer (Listening beyond Words)

Have you ever been in love? At first, you want to be with the other person all the time. What you do together doesn't seem to matter—talking incessantly about your feelings or just sitting quietly holding hands is enough. Just the physical presence of the other is fulfilling. That's how it is with God. But the difference is that God is with us *always*, even though we're not always aware of it. We're not tuned in. We see the world as physically separate from God. But just as the air we breathe is all around and inside us, but unseen, so is God. Feeling the presence of God, the one who loves you fully, is like taking a deep breath and filling your entire being.

"Be still, and know that I am God" (Psalm 46:10).

Centering prayer is a prayer of quieting and stillness that lets us know the presence of God in our innermost parts. It tunes our ears to the radio waves we can't see. It's a prayer without words and a journey to the center of our being.

Centering prayer had its beginnings with the Desert Fathers and Mothers—Christians who lived in the deserts of Egypt during the fourth and fifth centuries and followed a life of solitude and self-discipline. This form of prayer was the primary way of prayer for monks for centuries and more people are becoming interested in it today, thanks to the writings of the modern-day Trappist monk, Thomas Keating.

The practice is very simple. If you've ever entered a church and sat down in quiet preparation for a service, you've begun the practice of centering prayer. Its simple form, however, hides how difficult it can be in practice—and its rich rewards.

A good image of how centering prayer works is to imagine you are entering a holy circle. The circle is separated from the busyness of the day and at the center is God. You journey in a continually circling spiral away from thought and noise of the day toward the center of yourself—and God. Keep this image of the circle in mind as you try centering prayer.

First, find a quiet and comfortable place to sit. Begin by choosing a sacred word that says you're giving God permission to be present and act within you. Common sacred words are "God," "Jesus," "Abba," or "Father." Choose a word that reflects the love of God, but one that suggests the fewest images either positive or negative. The idea is to empty yourself of thought. The word itself isn't important. It's just a word that indicates your readiness for God.

Activity: Centering prayer isn't described in detail in the Bible, but Jesus did go by himself to be alone and pray. Read chapter 14 of Matthew to identify such a time. Where did Jesus go to pray? What happened just before? Just afterward?

Close your eyes and introduce the sacred word gently. As thoughts, feelings, or images surface, gently acknowledge them and let them go. An image that may be helpful is a stream. As you see thoughts of the day approach, gently let them continue floating down the stream. Centering prayer is not a prayer of words, but a silent prayer to God, to whom "all hearts are open, all desires known, and from [whom] no secrets are hid" (Book of Common Prayer, 355). God knows our needs and answers our prayers before we even ask.

Your body may twitch or itch during centering prayer. This is your body's way of working through its stress. If this distracts you, repeat your sacred word gently. You don't have to say the word constantly. When you notice that your mind is wandering or thoughts are intruding, reintroduce the word. As you continue, you'll find a kind of peacefulness inside of you. Rest in that peace. Don't worry if thoughts interrupt that peace. If they do, gently say your sacred word and let the thoughts go by.

Practicing contemplative prayer for ten minutes a day is a good beginning. To mark your time, set a CD of quiet music to begin playing after ten minutes. Or set a timer to ring gently after ten minutes. When your time of stillness is over, come out of the center by reciting the Lord's Prayer.

The result of centering prayer is awareness of how deeply God longs for you, his beloved. Centering prayer is not meditation in a void. It's creating empty spaces within to allow the Holy Spirit to grow inside. You'll be amazed: Knowing God's love and presence deep inside of you will help you see God's presence in all of creation and respond with loving actions.

Mantras

Inviting God to be with you is the beginning of any prayer. Some people find saying **mantras**—sacred words or phrases repeated for a period of time—help quiet their body and mind and invite God to be present. Mantras can help you tune out the voices of the world and tune in to God's voice.

An example of a simple mantra is "Come Holy Spirit, Come." This simple mantra names the presence of the divine and invites him in. To prepare for this prayer, again find a quiet place to sit and get comfortable. Be sure to remain sitting up and attentive. You want to be relaxed so that you're aware, but not so relaxed that you fall asleep. Take a deep breath in and say "Come Holy Spirit." Say it aloud. Breathe out as you say the final "Come."

breathe in saying	Come Holy Spirit,
breathe out saying	come.

Repeat this cycle of breathing in and out with the words "Come Holy Spirit, come" for five minutes. At the end of your prayer, stay in the silence for a few minutes and notice where your heart leads you. As you end your time of prayer, thank God for your time together.

Activity: Who is the Holy Spirit? Look in the Catechism in your Book of Common Prayer for an answer.

Other common words for this prayer are: "Lord, Jesus Christ, son of God, have mercy on me, a sinner." These words are the **Jesus Prayer**.

breathe in saying	Lord Jesus Christ
breathe out saying	son of God
breathe out saying	have mercy on me
breathe in saying	a sinner

A final example is the **Trisagion**, a Latin word that means "thrice holy:" Holy God, Holy and Mighty, Holy Immortal One, Have mercy on me.

breathe in saying	Holy God
breathe out saying	Holy and Mighty
breathe in saying	Holy Immortal One
breathe out saying	Have mercy on me

Once you are familiar with the Jesus Prayer and the Trisagion and these become part of your memory, you may be surprised how easily the words come to you when you need God's help.

The Jesus Prayer, the Trisagion, and other prayers like the words "Come, Holy Spirit, come," invite God and Jesus Christ to be present in our hearts. By repeating the words of invitation, your heart and mind will begin to empty, leaving room for the Holy Spirit to grow.

The result of this prayer is intimacy with God, a closeness that reveals that God provides for every need. For some the gift of this prayer is knowing that we're loved, for others protection from evil, and for still others the depth of love that gives us permission to reveal our sins and be forgiven. Each of us has a unique and important relationship with God that is deepened through prayer.

If it's difficult to remain physically still for longer than five minutes at a time, that's okay. We are, after all, physical beings. If you quickly become restless, you might find it helpful to use Anglican prayer beads along with a mantra.

Anglican Prayer Beads

Anglican prayer beads—sometimes called a rosary—are a set of thirty-three beads joined together into a circular pattern. You hold them in your hands and say sacred words as you travel with your fingers around the string of beads. Because it adds a physical element to prayer, the rosary engages our mind, spirit, and body. Fingering successive beads focuses our sometimes fidgety hands and links that focus to the words of our lips. In addition, the structure of the rosary and repetitive action of the beads creates a rhythm for prayer that stills our hearts.

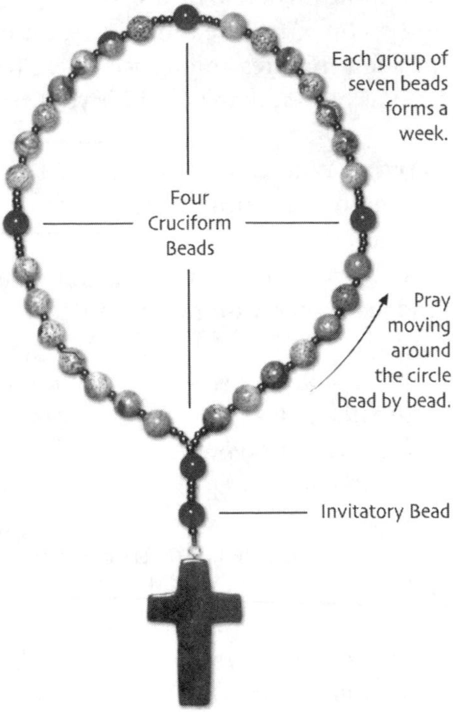

Anglican prayer beads are a way to include your body in prayer. (Credit: Full Circle Beads; fullcirclebeads.com)

Where Beads Come from and What They Symbolize

Beads were first used for prayer in the second century B.C.E. by followers of the Hindu faith as a way of counting prayers. The practice spread to Buddhism, Islam, and finally to Christianity. In the mid-sixteenth century, Pope Pius V decreed that Saint Dominic, founder of the Dominican Order, invented the rosary and the classic form for the Catholic rosary. Leaders of the Protestant Reformation discouraged the use of the rosary for devotions, and today rosaries are most commonly associated with Roman Catholics. The pattern we know as Anglican prayer beads developed in the 1980s. It has a cross, an invitatory bead, and twenty-eight beads divided into four weeks by four cruciform beads.

The word "Anglican" refers to things that relate to the Church of England and other churches that find their roots with the Church of England. The Episcopal Church in the United States is Anglican.

The structure of Anglican prayer beads is rich with symbolism that connects our prayer with time and space. There are four groups of seven beads, and each is called a *week*. The number seven reminds us of the seven days of our week, the seven days of creation, and the seven sacraments. In Jewish and Christian tradition, the number seven represents perfection and completion. The weeks are divided by four larger beads called *cruciform beads.* The four cruciform beads form the points of a cross, reminding us that by Jesus' death and resurrection we are freed from the power of sin and reconciled to God. Dividing the beads into groups of four also reminds us of the four seasons of the year and the four directions on a compass. The circular pattern symbolizes a journey and reminds us that the cycles of life—joy, sorrow, birth, and death—often repeat themselves.

In Anglican prayer beads, earthly and divine symbols are intertwined, reminding us that our faith involves our bodies too. God came to earth as a human being to be among us. Jesus suffered on the cross and rose from the dead. We live out our faith as the body of Christ in the world—a physical world with days, seasons, geography—all made sacred by God.

Did You Know?

The modern word "bead" comes from the old English word *bede,* meaning prayer. A *bedesman* was someone whose duty it was to pray for others.

Praying with the Beads

Prayer beads are used along with words. Before you begin, choose four simple prayers. Two of the prayers are said as you enter the circle—one for the cross and another for the invitatory, or first, bead. A simple prayer for the cross is, "In the Name of God the Father, Son and Holy Spirit, Amen." You might try using the Trisagion for the invitatory bead and the cruciform beads and the Jesus Prayer for the weeks. As you enter the circle, move to the right, saying the Jesus Prayer for each of the seven beads, followed by the Trisagion for the cruciform bead, and returning to the Jesus Prayer. Going around three times before ending with the invitatory and cross represents the Trinity of the Father, Son and Holy Spirit. By the end of three rounds, you will have said one hundred prayers. More than that, you'll find your heart to be still and your mind to be at rest. Before completing your time of prayer, spend some time in silence and thank God for your time together.

Activity: Find the Trisagion in your Book of Common Prayer on page 324. Why do you think it appears at this part of the Eucharist?

Remember, prayer beads are meant to help your prayer. At first, remembering the prayer might be difficult and the beads might be confusing. Relax.

Start with simple prayers and perhaps only two—one for the weeks and another for the other beads. With practice you'll become more comfortable. And trust your intuition. You may find that other prayer practices work better to create the space where you and God can meet.

Lectio Divina

As Christians we believe that the Bible is the revealed word of God. God inspired human authors, who wrote the texts through which God speaks. So, a natural place to listen for God's voice is the Bible. People read the Bible in many ways—for its literary value, for instruction, and for inspiration. The first two kinds of reading use the human intellect and invite us to study the history, language, and setting of the bible stories. The third way requires that we listen with our hearts to what the Word of God is saying to each of us personally at a particular moment.

One way of deep listening to Scripture is *lectio divina*. ***Lectio divina*** is a four-step way of prayerfully reading the Word of God. Saint Benedict, a Christian monk who lived in the fifth century C.E. and believed reading and study is a central part of a sacred life, encouraged the widespread practice of *lectio divina*.

Lectio divina has four steps: reading, meditating, praying, and contemplating. To begin, find a place where you can listen to yourself and to God and select a brief passage from the Bible. Quiet your body and your mind with slow breathing. Perhaps say a mantra. (See page 120.)

Lectio divina are Latin words for divine reading.

Website pray-as-you-go.org offers a daily *lectio divina* meditation in mp3 file format for portable audio players.

Read. Read the passage slowly, savoring each word and allowing the words to reach your inner self. Ask yourself, "What word or phrase is speaking to me right now?" During this step you're seeking God's still small voice that speaks to you softly, gently, and in love.

Meditate. Take that word for yourself and recite it over and over again. This step is meditation. Let your heart open itself to that word. It's a gift from God. Let your thoughts and imagination play with the word. What images does the word suggest? What thoughts or desires surface within you? By meditating on the word God has given you, you find the word to be part of you.

Pray. Now let the word touch you deeply. Pray with the word. What feelings and emotions does this word bring to your mind? Hold up these feelings and repeat the word or phrase. Hold yourself up to God and ask for God's healing grace and guidance.

Contemplate. Finally, rest in God's love. Accept God's loving embrace. Enjoy God's presence and thank God for the gift you've received. This final step is called contemplation.

Lectio divina isn't meant to replace the study of Scripture. Studying Scripture with commentaries helps us understand the communities and times when stories and poetry in the Bible were written. It helps us interpret the Bible in context and with the insights of scholars. The process of *lectio divina* can also be used with a poem, a picture, something in nature, or a life event. God continues to speak to us today through the created world as well as through the Bible. Follow the four steps of *lectio divina*, but instead of focusing on a word, focus on the subject you've chosen. By doing this you can begin to see all of God's creation as sacred.

Activity: Read Psalm 121 from your Book of Common Prayer using the method of *lectio divina*. What word or words spoke to you today?

Praying through Icons

Some people like to use visual images when they pray, and icons are great images to pray with. **Icons** are visual images that point beyond themselves. They can be powerful instruments that instruct us, changing our behavior and attitude. The Nike logo, with its message "just do it," is just one of the many icons in our culture. It tells us to get moving and do something. The image of George Washington printed on a dollar bill is another American icon. That icon tells us that this little green piece of paper has value. We can give it to a clerk at a store and the clerk will give us a product we've chosen. By themselves, icons have no power. Their power is in what they represent or point to. George Washington's image on the dollar represents trust—trust that this piece of paper can be exchanged for something else at the mall. Icons are everywhere. Other familiar icons are the ones on your computer screen.

The Nike logo is an icon. Its meaning isn't in the image, but in what it represents—power and action.

"Icon" is the Greek word for image.

Did You Know?

Tradition has it that a woman named Veronica offered Jesus a cloth on his way to the cross on which to wipe his face. When he returned the cloth, his image remained on the cloth. The name Veronica means "true image."

"Clicking" on these icons launches powerful programs that perform many functions.

Holy icons are similar. They point beyond themselves to the Holy and lead us into the presence of God. Traditional icons are beautiful paintings of Jesus, Mary, and the saints—holy men and women who have gone before us. These icons are "written" by artists in prayer. Find an icon. Notice it has an inner light that invites you to gaze at it patiently and prayerfully. As you look at the icon, it can move your heart to recognize how beautiful the world is and how loving God must be to have created such a beautiful world.

Icons don't have to be painted. Nature is filled with icons that point to God, our creator: a dandelion, a blade of grass, a bird's nest. Although all of them serve a purpose in nature, they can also serve as icons that point beyond themselves to their creator. Taking the time to read these icons can show us the beauty of creation. Consider the six-sided honeycomb. The fact that it both incubates bees and stores food with mathematical beauty reveals a creator of amazing complexity and creativity.

How can you pray through an icon? First select an icon—either by going to where it is (in nature) or by bringing it to a sacred place indoors. Make it the focus of your attention. Begin by quieting your body, mind and spirit. Ask God to be present and focus on the beauty and inner life of the icon. What is the icon saying about itself? What is it saying about God? What feeling does the icon evoke in you? Focus on and rest on this feeling. Respond to God as you feel moved to—with adoration, confession,

Religious icons point beyond themselves to God. This icon of St. Francis of Assisi is written by Robert Lentz, OFM (1987). (Courtesy of Trinity Stores, www.trinitystores.com, 800-699-4482.)

thanksgiving, intercession, or praise. End with a familiar prayer such as the Lord's Prayer.

PRAYING WITH YOUR BODY

So far, we've talked about prayer without words, prayer with words, and prayer with images. In each of these practices—except praying with Anglican prayer beads—our bodies haven't been active participants. We're physical beings and God loves all of who we are, so our worship and prayer practices should reflect that fact. For example, during our worship together we kneel or stand for prayer. Many make the sign of the cross and bow as the cross processes by.

Activity: Open your prayer book to the service of Holy Eucharist most familiar to you. Go through the service, listing how you use your body in each part. What feelings or thoughts do you associate with each action?

These motions hold **ritual memory**—the remembrance of actions that deepen our experiences as they are repeated. An example of ritual memory is kneeling in prayer. Try it. Because we've done it so often, the act of kneeling places our minds and bodies in the context of prayer. By kneeling our bodies remember other times we have knelt—the emotions, smells, sights, and sounds that surrounded us while kneeling. Ritual memory is powerful. So, be mindful of your body and prayer. The following practices engage your body in prayer.

> Our bodies hold memories. Try kneeling or posing as if you are praying and see how it changes how you feel.

Mandalas

Creating visual images while we invite God to be present can be a powerful way to pray. Being creative with our hands focuses our minds and hearts and allows us to explore our innermost selves. Many people reveal themselves best through visual media.

One visual method of prayer is to draw a **mandala**, a circular pattern of lines and colors. You can find mandalas throughout nature. The cell with its nucleus, the nautilus, the earth seen from space, the pattern of our spiraling galaxy, and even the atom are all mandalas. The stained glass rose windows in many churches and the labyrinth are also mandalas. The circle creates a safe place where we can be with God.

Mandalas have a long history. The practice of creating mandalas originated with Buddhist monks in ancient Tibet, who created intricate circular

A mystic is someone who experiences God directly through union with or revelation from God.

patterns with sand. The word "mandala" comes from the Sanskrit word meaning circle. Twelfth-century German mystic Hildegard von Bingen, known for her visions and musical and artistic abilities, created many mandalas.

To begin drawing a mandala, take a large blank sheet of paper and with a compass draw a large circle. Actively invite God to the circle and to your prayer. Let your thoughts and emotions suggest a color and pattern and begin to draw. Let your imagination go with pencils, paints, crayons, magic markers, and other drawing tools. Draw what comes to mind—there is no "right" or "wrong" mandala. Each mandala is unique. Empty yourself into the circle, offering your worries, thoughts, hopes, and desires to God.

Drawing a mandala is a way of paying attention to your inner self. When you've finished your mandala, look at it as a whole to see what themes emerge. Where is God in the pattern of the mandala? After thinking about it for a little while, give thanks to God for calling you to his presence.

Journaling

Journaling is a discipline of putting our thoughts on paper for reflection, self-examination, and prayer. It can be a way of helping us to be honest with ourselves.

This is a mandala painted by mystic Hildegard von Bingen called the Tree of Life (twelfth century).

Like many young girls and boys, when I was a teenager I had a little diary with a lock. The lock suggested that these were to be my precious thoughts—nobody else's. And that's true. The only problem was, the lined pages, headed with the days of the week, suggested schoolwork and implied that I *had* to write in it every day. The excitement of writing something every day soon became a burden. Today, that diary is almost empty.

Just a few years ago, I thought I'd try journaling again. I needed to make sense of where my life was going, work out complicated thoughts and feelings, and understand what God was calling me to do. I found a beautiful leather-covered journal with a Celtic design on the cover and *blank* pages inside. The blank pages freed me from expectations and thoughts of schoolwork. And the beauty of the book showed me that my life was sacred and deserved to be written about.

Journals are meant to free the soul, and I began to fill up the blank pages of my journal with words, drawings, and doodles. Stories and feelings poured out, reflecting my innermost hopes, fears, anger, and love. They were honest and meant only for my eyes.

Every person has an inner voice. Sometimes we can hear it clearly. Journaling can often help us to hear it better.

As with any kind of prayer, journaling is personal. You can journal in spiral-bound notebooks, on the computer, or in a scrapbook. Begin by inviting God to your journaling. Write what comes to mind. Be honest, even if it's painful or you think God doesn't want to hear it. Without honesty you can't truly face yourself or God. Writing will help you find your true voice. Seeing your thoughts written on paper gives them greater importance. Try it. Also, by writing down your thoughts you can read them again later. You might notice that your thoughts aren't what you remembered. Reading past thoughts will help you recognize how your thoughts change.

Try journaling with images. Perhaps journaling with mandalas will help you journey to your inner self. God speaks to us through our lives. Ask yourself where God is in your journal. What is God saying to you? Journaling can help you see your life and offer it to God.

The labyrinth is a mandala that you walk to pray. Source: Veriditas (veriditas.net). Used with permission.

Walking a Labyrinth

A **labyrinth** is a sacred pattern in the shape of a circle with one path that winds to the center and back out again. With its circular shape of a mandala, the labyrinth reflects the unity and wholeness of creation and our lives.

A very famous labyrinth is the eleven-circuit labyrinth on the floor of the Chartres Cathedral in

France. This labyrinth was built in the twelfth century for Christian pilgrimages. The Crusades had made pilgrimages to holy places such as Jerusalem, Rome, and Santiago dangerous, so the church made seven cathedrals in France, including Chartres, alternative pilgrimage destinations. When they arrived there, pilgrims would walk the labyrinth before receiving the Eucharist.

Labyrinth designs actually date back to 2500 B.C.E. and are found in many religions and cultures.

Lauren Artress, a priest at Grace Cathedral in San Francisco, led the installation of the eleven-circuit labyrinth at the Cathedral and in the 1990s founded the modern labyrinth movement. Today, you can find labyrinths in nearly every major American city. Smaller finger labyrinths are available for people who are either unable to walk or do not have access to floor labyrinths.

Just like any journey, walking a labyrinth can change you. Once you enter the labyrinth, you begin a journey that takes you to the center and out again. You focus on taking the next step on the path with God, without worrying about the destination. Unlike a maze, which is designed to make us lost and confused, a labyrinth has no wrong turns and no dead-ends. Because you don't have to use your brain to walk the labyrinth successfully, you can free your heart to listen to God. People who have walked labyrinths often say they find that God has given them an answer to important questions while they were on their labyrinth journey.

A labyrinth is a symbol for life with a loving God who doesn't deceive us or lead us astray. Walking the labyrinth is a journey with a God who beckons us along the journey to holiness.

Fasting

Fasting is actively choosing not to do something for a short period of time so that we may draw our attention toward God. Fasting is a way of developing self-control and emptying ourselves. When Jesus lived, fasting was a regular practice among Jews. In the Gospel according to Matthew, Jesus fasted from food before beginning his ministry. Today, Lent—the days leading up to Easter—is a common time for Christians to practice the discipline of fasting.

Consider taking on the discipline of fasting during Lent. Think of something you really love to do, but can continue to live healthfully without. Some families fast from watching television and instead play board games and set aside time for Evening Prayer. Episcopal author Lauren Winner loves to read novels. She always has a book in her hand. Reading is a good thing. One year, however, she decided to give up reading novels for

Lent. Every time she reached for a book, she stopped and instead reached out to God. She thanked God for the ability to read and remembered that she needs God just as much as she needs a book to read. By fasting, we give up our physical attachment to material things and, just as in centering prayer, allow the Holy Spirit to dwell in our hearts. What each of us is called to fast from depends on what we do. Remember, fasting is meant to *improve* our spiritual health. Perhaps fasting from video games or instant messaging will provide you with time for God. It's not a time to deprive our bodies or cause bodily harm. Instead, fasts free us through prayer to center on God. By removing an activity from our lives, we allow our spiritual needs to take priority. In the metaphor of tuning the radio, fasting is like clearing away the white noise in the world to hear God's signal more clearly.

Both fasting and feasting are spiritual disciplines.

CELEBRATION

Remember the excitement of waking up to the celebration of your birthday? Maybe someone cooked a special breakfast, made you a cake, and gave you brightly wrapped gifts. Celebration, or feasting, is a way we mark life events. Celebration is also a spiritual discipline and part of a life of prayer.

The forty days of Lent in which many practice fasting is followed by fifty days of Easter, a time of great celebration. After Jesus fasted for forty days, angels descended to minister to him. Celebration is a fundamental spiritual discipline. Does this surprise you? It shouldn't.

The very word "gospel" means good news. In the Gospel of John, the first of the signs Jesus performed of the coming of the kingdom of God was to turn water into wine at the wedding in Cana. Jesus uses the image of a banquet to describe God's kingdom. And in the face of his coming death, Jesus celebrates Passover, the liberation of the Jews from the Egyptians, with his closest friends. The conquest over death and the coming of the reign of God is cause for celebration! The Eucharist that we celebrate every Sunday is, in fact, a celebration, and *the* central act of the church.

Activity: In your Book of Common Prayer, find the sections "The Calendar of the Church Year" and the services in "Proper Liturgies for Special Days." What are the principal feasts of the church?

What marks celebration as a spiritual and prayerful act is that it's an intentional act of praise and thanksgiving that reflects our joy with God in creation. We acknowledge God's presence and mark the day with special foods and close friends.

Lesser Feasts and Fasts suggests opportunities for celebrating. It lists the church calendar with feast days that commemorate events of the life of Jesus as well as the lives of men and women who have dedicated their lives to active witness of God. This book includes collects, psalms, and lessons that you can read as part of celebrations. You might incorporate prayers and readings into the celebrations of God's abundance into *your* life.

Parents and Mentors

Share with one another how you pray. Do you have a favorite time to pray? Or a favorite prayer? Commit to praying for one another during the next few weeks.

RULE OF LIFE

Leading a spiritual life means developing an *ongoing* relationship with God. This chapter offers lots of spiritual disciplines to help you develop that relationship. But which ones will be good for *you*? How will they fit in with all the other things you have to do? Leading a spiritual life doesn't mean kneeling all day in prayer, or constantly drawing mandalas. We need to live balanced lives with God at the center.

Maintaining a balance, or even knowing what balance is, isn't easy. Demands by others and by our egos get in the way. A helpful way to find and maintain balance is to develop a rule of life. A **rule of life** is a set of guidelines for living that help us keep our lives in balance with God as the center.

A rule of life can help us keep our lives in balance with God as the center. The Rule of Saint Benedict, written in the sixth century, is a rule of life that balances work, study, and prayer.

Monastic communities live today—as they have for centuries—by rules of life. The best known rule of life is the Rule of Saint Benedict, written by Benedict of Nursia in the sixth century. The Rule of Saint Benedict balances work, study, and prayer and shows monks how to live together.

When a person joins a monastic community he or she vows to follow a rule of life that is different from other rules of life. For one, not everybody is called to a life of poverty or chastity, both common vows in monastic communities. Each of us is called by God into a particular rule. Writer Debra Farrington suggests that a way to begin to develop your rule of life is to write a list of activities that bring you joy.[1] It may include running, writing, drawing, reading, or

1. The categories of a rule of life and steps of creating rules are loosely based on "Balancing Life by the Rule" by Debra Farrington in *Spirituality & Health* (Winter 2001), 44.

spending time alone. This list is the beginning of your rule of life. Put your activities into five categories: work, study, prayer, play, and service to others. For most of you work is school and homework. Study might be reading the Bible or books about the Christian tradition.

Bring this list to God and pray for guidance. You may begin to recognize some activities as being spiritual for the first time. Running, for example, takes care of one's body and therefore is a way of returning the blessing of health to God. Time with friends creates community of love and support. You may want to re-balance some parts of your life. If so, take on a discipline that is reasonable. A rule of life is a realistic set of guidelines.

Keep your rule of life handy. It will help you remain accountable and help you see when the rule needs to be modified. A rule of life is a living structure and will change. Most of all, a rule of life, by intentionally making God the center of your life, is a blessing that can bring you into closer relationship to God.

Activity: The Apostle Paul lists the fruit of leading a spiritual life in Galatians 5:22–23. What are they?

SPIRITUAL DIRECTION

Some people find spiritual direction helpful in developing an awareness of God in their lives. **Spiritual direction** is the art of helping others explore a deeper relationship with God. Spiritual directors are trained to listen deeply to others and to help people listen to God and learn where God is leading them. They can help you develop an awareness of God in your life and help you discern what spiritual disciplines will bring you closer to God. They are not therapists or problem solvers. They are holy listeners and wise people who can, with God, provide guidance in creating a life of spiritual discipline that brings the seeker into an ever-closer presence with God.

DEVELOPING YOUR SPIRITUALITY

There are many more spiritual practices we didn't explore—retreats, simplicity, study, and service are just a few. With all of the possibilities of spiritual practices, you might wonder, "Where do I begin?" Begin where your heart leads you. Begin with a prayer of petition from Psalm 19:14,

> Let the words of my mouth and the meditation of my heart be
> acceptable in your sight,
> O Lord, my rock and my redeemer.

Remember the parable of the sower in Matthew 13 and Mark 4? A sower sowed seeds. Some fell on a path and the birds ate them up. Some fell on rocky ground. They sprang up but the soil was too shallow and the plants withered. Other seeds fell among thorns and the thorns choked the plants. Some seeds fell on good soil and grew into an abundant harvest. By tilling our lives and cultivating the spirit, God's love and blessings will grow in abundance. The fruits of the Spirit—love, joy, peace, patience, kindness, goodness, and faith—will be plentiful.

Chapter 8

Navigating the Church: From Parish to Worldwide Church

When the day of Pentecost had come, they were all together in one place. And suddenly from heaven there came a sound like the rush of a violent wind, and it filled the entire house where they were sitting. (Acts 2:1–2)

Fifty days after Passover, the twelve apostles gathered to celebrate a harvest festival called Shavuot, also called Pentecost. During their gathering, the Holy Spirit came upon the apostles, and tongues of fire rested on each of them. The Holy Spirit gave them the ability to spread the gospel in many languages throughout the nations. On that day thousands of people repented of their sins and were baptized. The church was born. Every year, fifty days after Easter, on Pentecost Sunday, we recall that day—the birth of the church—with readings and the color red to represent the fire of the Holy Spirit.

Immediately before his ascension, Jesus told the apostles and other followers to be his "witnesses in Jerusalem, in all Judea and Samaria, and to the ends of the earth" (Acts 1:8). Representing Christ in the world is still the central ministry of the church.

ONE, HOLY, CATHOLIC, AND APOSTOLIC

As you read in Chapter 3, the Episcopal Church in the United States was established in 1789. About seventeen hundred years or so earlier on

Pentecost the church was born. As we say each Sunday with the words of the Nicene Creed, the church that was born on Pentecost is "the one, holy, catholic, and apostolic Church." By *one* we mean that the church is one body with Christ as its head. All denominations are not the same, but all worship the same God. By *holy* we mean that the Holy Spirit dwells among us and continues to guide us in representing Christ in the world. By **catholic** (lowercase c) we mean universal—our faith is a faith for all people and for all time. God intended the church to be for all nations, for the wealthy and poor alike, for both men and women, and for people of every social class and level of education. In the Prayers of the People each week, we pray for the whole church, all Christian people. The church is **apostolic** because the church continues in the teaching and community that the apostles began in the years after Jesus' death and resurrection. Just after the baptism of thousands on Pentecost, the writer of the Acts of the Apostles tells us that the newly baptized "devoted themselves to the apostles' teaching and fellowship, to the breaking of bread and the prayers." The church continues those central actions and has an unbroken history from its birth on Pentecost to the present day.

We believe in the one, holy, catholic, and apostolic Church.

As a whole and in its parts, the church is the community of people who, at baptism, renounced evil and turned to Jesus Christ as their Savior. The church is a people who believe in God the Father, God the Son, and God the Holy Spirit. The Episcopal Church is part of the one, holy, catholic, and apostolic church.

Activity: How is the church described in the Bible? See the Catechism on page 854 in the Book of Common Prayer.

THE CHURCH AS ONE

Ever eat honey from the comb? As you chew the wax combs, sweet nectar, turned to dense honey, squeezes out into your mouth. A delight! For a few years, my father tended honey bee hives for our family—just enough for peanut butter–and–honey sandwiches for our family and French toast and honey for my preschool class on their visit to see the bees.

Bee colonies are amazing. For starters, their homes are a beautiful arrangement of six-sided cells that fit perfectly together. But more than the beauty of their homes is their behavior. Bees act in a colony as if they were a single organism. Each has a specific role to play that keeps the entire community healthy. One queen bee lays eggs all day. Depending on their stage of life, worker bees take care of the larvae (the newly hatched baby bees), clean house, or forage for food. Drones mate with virgin queens from other colonies to pass along their colony's genes. The colony's survival depends on each bee fulfilling its duties. Bees are so committed to their colony that they will give up their lives to protect it. A honey bee that stings dies as soon as it's done.

Just like a bee hive, the church is a living organism with thousands of members, each with its own role to play. When working well, the hive acts as one with one mission: "to restore all people to unity with God and each other in Christ." The church needs each of its members to carry out this mission and it needs these members to act in a coordinated way. In this chapter we'll look at how the Episcopal Church in the United States is coordinated—its structure, the rules by which it acts, and the way its decisions are made.

Just like a bee hive, the church is a living organism with thousands of members, each with his or her own role to play.

YOU AND THE OTHER MINISTERS

As a candidate for confirmation, you're probably baptized. (If you aren't, you will be before being confirmed.) And, because baptism is full initiation into the body of Christ, you are also a *full* member of the church. Nothing more is needed to complete your membership. You don't need to pass a test. At your baptism you were already marked as Christ's own forever. As a member of the body of Christ, you're also a *minister* of the church; that is, you're called to serve others on behalf of Christ. This broad definition of minister may surprise you. Most people reserve the word "minister" for the ordained. But because each member of the church is called to live out the promises made at baptism, each member has a ministry and so is a minister of the church.

The ministers of the church include lay persons, bishops, priests, and deacons. While all ministers share the basic ministry of representing Jesus and his church, each person is called in a different way to fulfill that ministry. **Laypersons** find their ministry working and acting out in the world as students, workers, parents, community activists, and so on. The remaining three ministries are ordained ministries.

Laypersons are the people of the church who are baptized. The ministry of laypeople is mainly out in the world while the ministry of priests is mainly within the church.

We discussed the specific ministries of each of three Holy Orders in Chapter 6. In the next chapter we explore the ministry of the laity. Here's a brief reminder of each of the Holy Orders. Bishops serve as apostle, chief priest, and pastor of a diocese. Priests lead parishes as a pastor to the people. Deacons perform a special ministry of serving the needs of others, especially the poor, the sick, and the suffering. Deacons also assist a priest or bishop in worship. Laypersons, bishops, priests, and deacons are all ministers in the Episcopal Church.

Activity: What is the duty of all Christians? See page 856 in the Book of Common Prayer.

THE EPISCOPAL CHURCH OF THE UNITED STATES

The Episcopal Church is comprised of about 2.5 million baptized members in 7,200 churches and missions, 300 bishops, 14,000 priests, and nearly 2,000 deacons throughout the United States, Latin America, the Caribbean, Taiwan, and Europe. (Latin American and Caribbean countries included in the Episcopal Church are Colombia, Dominican Republic, Ecuador, Haiti, Honduras, Puerto Rico, the Virgin Islands, and Venezuela. The Episcopal Church in Europe is comprised of American churches whose membership is made up mostly of Americans living abroad, for example those in the military, in business, or studying in a foreign country.)

The Episcopal Church is usually considered a Protestant Church, meaning that it's distinct from the Roman Catholic and the Eastern Orthodox Churches. About 25 percent of Americans identify themselves as Roman Catholic and 50 percent as Protestant. About 1 percent of Americans are members of the Episcopal Church. About half of all Episcopalians belong to a parish with 200 or more members. And a few have members numbering in the thousands. About 16,000 young people and 18,000 adults are confirmed in the Episcopal Church each year.

While the Episcopal Church is generally categorized as Protestant, Episcopalians understand themselves as both Protestant and Catholic—Protestant because its members worship in our own language, use a Book of Common Prayer, and rely on Scripture, reason, and tradition to interpret the Bible; and Catholic because it upholds the faith of the early church through sacraments and creeds.

Structure of the Church: A Bird's Eye View

A helpful way to get a handle on the way the Episcopal Church is governed is to look at its parallels to U.S. government. The following table shows the similarities.

Parallels between the United States Government and the Episcopal Church

Nation .... Episcopal Church
President........................ Presiding Bishop
Congress .... General Convention
Senate.......................... House of Bishops
House of Representatives ...... House of Deputies

State............................ Diocese
Governor........................ Bishop
State Legislature .... Diocesan Convention

City .... Parish
Mayor........................... Rector
City Council.................... Vestry

Just as the U.S. government has three levels of government—federal, state, and local—the Episcopal Church is divided into three levels, too—churchwide, diocesan, and parish, each with its own elected leader. The Presiding Bishop is the leader of the Episcopal Church; bishops lead dioceses; and rectors lead parishes. Just as with U.S. government, each level of the church government has its own law-making body. The Episcopal Church is governed by two houses—the House of Bishops and the House of Deputies. You probably recognize the parallels with the two houses of the U.S. Congress, as shown above.

The Shield of the Episcopal Church was adopted in 1940. Its design recognizes our history. The nine white crosses symbolize the nine dioceses that met at the first General Convention in 1789 and ratified the original constitution. They are arranged in the form of the cross of Saint Andrew, the patron saint of Scotland. The red cross is the Cross of Saint George, the patron saint of the Church of England.

Activity: How does the church pursue its mission and through whom does it carry out this mission? See the Catechism on page 855 of the Book of Common Prayer.

Your Church

So far we know that the universal church is made up of all baptized Christians, but what about the church where you worship, study, pray, and meet friends? Most of the 7,200 churches in the Episcopal Church are **parishes**—self-supporting communities that worship regularly together. A priest who leads the parish is called its **rector**. Rectors are elected by the vestry, the governing body of the parish, and confirmed by the bishop of the diocese.

Members of a Parish

Although all baptized persons are members of the church, the particular parish you belong to depends on Episcopal Church rules. When you were baptized, your name was recorded as a member of that parish. You officially became a *member of record*. If you change parishes, you can transfer your membership by requesting a *letter of transfer* from your original parish.

The **Constitution and Canons of the Episcopal Church**, the written rules that govern the Episcopal Church, recognize members who are sixteen years old and older as adult members. Whether this is sufficient for voting at a particular parish depends on that parish's by-laws and the laws of the state. Not everyone who attends church becomes a formal member of a parish, and not all formal members attend regularly. **Communicants** are members who have had Holy Communion at least three times in the previous year. A **communicant in good standing** is a communicant who has been ". . . faithful in working, praying, and giving for the spread of the Kingdom of God" (Constitution and Canons of Episcopal Church).

> Like the U.S. government, the Episcopal Church has laws. These laws are called canons. The rules of most parishes are established in by-laws.

Governance of a Parish

The way a parish is governed depends on the laws of each diocese and state, as well as on the parish's by-laws, the written rules that set out how a parish is governed. Every year, a parish has an annual meeting when members discuss plans for the coming year and share their concerns. At this meeting, members usually vote on the parish budget and elect members of the vestry. They also elect delegates to the Diocesan Convention.

Because it's difficult for every single member of the church to get together to discuss all the issues of running the parish, they elect a small group, called a **vestry**, to supervise and make decisions about the finances and buildings and grounds between annual meetings. The size of the vestry, term of office, and requirements for election depend on the by-laws of the parish and in some cases the laws of the state.

The church membership or the vestry elects two officers—a senior warden and a junior warden—either from among its members or from the vestry. In some parishes, the rector selects the senior warden. Traditionally the senior warden acts as a link between the rector and the parish, while the junior warden supervises the buildings and grounds of the parish. The rector presides at vestry meetings, unless he or she asks the senior warden to do so.

Activity: Attend a vestry meeting. Who are the junior and senior wardens at your parish?

Every church has by-laws. These laws, adopted by the members of the parish, determine such things as who is eligible for election to the vestry, how officers are elected, and when the annual meeting is held. The by-laws of a church must be consistent with the canons (rules) of its diocese and the Episcopal Church.

Mission and Ministry

The Catechism in the Book of Common Prayer tells us that the mission of the church is "to restore all people to unity with God and each other in Christ." It doesn't say anything about buildings, clergy, vestries, or budgets! But all those ordinary details help the church carry out its primary mission. Vestries oversee budgets, the clergy lead worship, committees carry out the work of Christian education and community service. In the next chapter we will carefully explore the ministry of the church. For now, let's continue to look at the way the church organization helps make that ministry happen.

Your Diocese

The Episcopal Church isn't a congregational church—it acts not on its own but as part of a **diocese** led by a bishop. A diocese is the basic unit of the Episcopal Church. Individual churches act within the rules of the diocese—and share a common mission.

Your diocese is one of 110 dioceses in the Episcopal Church (100 domestic and 10 international), which range in size from 20 or 30 to

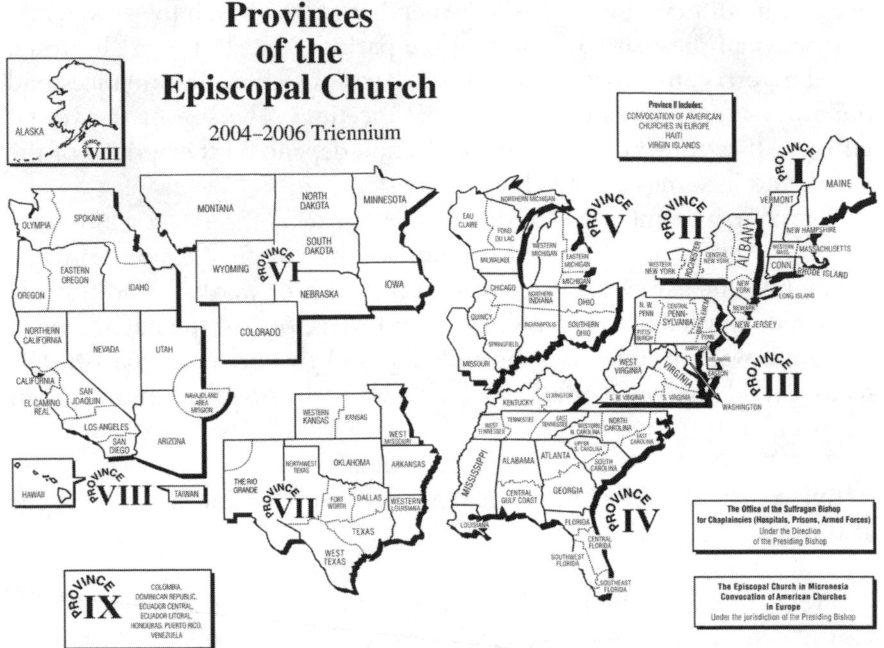

The Episcopal Church is divided into nine provinces. Some provinces include dioceses in foreign countries. (Courtesy of The Domestic and Foreign Missionary Society of the Protestant Episcopal Church.)

almost 200 churches. The largest domestic diocese is the Diocese of Massachusetts (one of two in the state of Massachusetts), with 194 churches and about 70,000 members. The smallest diocese is the Diocese of Eau Claire (one of three in Wisconsin), with 19 churches and fewer than 3,000 members. Many dioceses cover an entire state. Others, in densely populated states, cover only portions of a state. The state of New York, for example, is made up of six dioceses, while the entire state of Wyoming is one diocese.

Each parish contributes to the diocese to pay for the salary of the bishop and diocesan staff and to help run diocesan programs, including the Domestic and Foreign Missionary Society of the Episcopal Church. Members of parishes also serve on diocesan committees and participating in and lead ministries such as retreats for teenagers.

Your Bishop

Your bishop is an ordained priest and serves as the chief priest and pastor of the church in the geographic region that your diocese covers. In the early church, a bishop (in Greek, *episcopos* means overseer) was an elder appointed by a community of believers. As Christian communities grew, bishops began to lead other parishes close by as well as their own. The responsibilities of a bishop continue to be to oversee and supervise the churches in the diocese and to serve as pastor to the clergy and their families.

Activity: Which services can be led only by a bishop? Refer to the page before each service, titled "Concerning the . . ." in the Book of Common Prayer.

Bishops have authority over matters of faith, discipline, and worship within his or her diocese. Bishops ordain priests and deacons, consecrate other bishops, confirm those who wish to receive the sacrament of confirmation (confirmands), and preside at their diocesan conventions. Bishops represent the connection of all parishes within a diocese, the connection of all dioceses to one another, and the connection of the church today with the early Christian church established by the apostles.

> Bishops represent unity within the diocese, unity with other dioceses in the national Episcopal Church, and unity with the history of apostles.

In most dioceses, one parish church serves as the diocese's **cathedral**. The word "cathedral" is derived from the word *cathedra*, or the teaching seat of the bishop and oldest sign of the authority of a bishop. It's similar to the county seat of government. A cathedral doesn't have to be a big, fancy church. In fact, the cathedral of the Diocese of Northern Virginia has no walls. It is an outdoor church whose roof is a canopy of trees in the Shenandoah Valley. What makes a church a cathedral is that it houses the bishop's cathedra. A cathedral is the principal church for the diocese and commonly hosts diocesan events and Episcopal services such as ordinations of priests and deacons and the consecration of a bishop. The lead clergyperson at a cathedral is called a **dean**; assisting clergy at a cathedral may be called **canons**.

The Diocesan Convention

Each year the diocese holds a **Diocesan Convention** of both laypeople and clergy. All clergy in a diocese, plus a number of elected lay ministers from each parish, are given a place to sit at the meetings, the opportunity to speak, and a ballot to vote. Some dioceses have additional youth representatives. (The number of laypeople that a parish sends generally depends on the size of the parish.) All representatives to convention, clergy and laity alike, elect officers to various commissions and councils of the diocese and vote on the diocesan budget, policies, and positions. They may also vote to change the Diocesan Constitution and Canons.

Activity: Get a copy of your diocese's canons. (Many are posted on diocesan websites.) How many delegates can your parish elect as deputies to the Diocesan Convention? Who is eligible to be elected?

Diocesan Constitution and Canons

Diocesan Constitution and Canons are similar to a parish's by-laws. They're the rules that govern a diocese. These rules determine things like starting new churches, dealing with churches whose membership is dwindling, electing a bishop, sending delegates to convention, choosing committees, making rules governing parish vestries, and deciding on the duties of diocesan officers. The Constitution and Canons are accepted and modified by Diocesan Convention, but they must always be consistent with the Constitution and Canons of the Episcopal Church.

Diocesan Council

Between conventions, the business of the diocese is coordinated by a **Diocesan Council**. Diocesan Councils are similar to vestries in a parish. They act on behalf of Diocesan Convention during the year. The Diocesan Council is usually made up of the bishop and other elected members, both clergy and lay.

Election of a Bishop

When a bishop dies, resigns, or is called to another ministry, a special Diocesan Convention is called to elect a new bishop. Usually a nominating committee is formed that reviews resumés and interviews candidates. Delegates to convention meet the candidates and vote on a bishop. Election usually requires a majority of both laypersons and clergy at the special convention. Just as a rector must be approved by the bishop, the election of a bishop must be confirmed by a majority of bishops in the Episcopal Church. A bishop is consecrated by three other bishops by the laying on of hands, which expresses our belief that the ministry of bishop is a gift of the Holy Spirit. The three bishops symbolize a continuous apostolic ministry and the communion of all Christian communities with one another.

Some dioceses are so large that one bishop can't serve all churches in the diocese alone, so they elect another bishop to help. The diocese can elect either a *bishop suffragan*, who can't become bishop or, with the consent of the bishop diocesan, a *bishop coadjutor* who succeeds the diocesan bishop. A bishop diocesan can also appoint a *bishop assisting*.

Companion Dioceses

Some dioceses in the Episcopal Church have developed companion relationships with other dioceses in the Anglican Communion. Over one hundred companion relationships exist today. Examples are the relationship between the Diocese of Bethlehem in Pennsylvania and Kajo Keji in the Sudan, and between the Diocese of California and the Beijing Christian Council of China. Companion dioceses usually pray for one another each week during worship, support one another financially, and may travel to one another's diocese to share experiences and learn from one another. Companion diocese relationships show the shared mission of all dioceses throughout the world—to restore all people to unity with God and each other in Christ.

Activity: Does your diocese have a companion relationship with another diocese? If so, with whom is the companion relationship?

Provinces

Dioceses are clustered geographically into nine provinces. The map on page 142 shows all nine provinces of the Episcopal Church. Notice that Province IX is churches in Central and South America. Each province holds leadership conferences twice a year to discuss common issues. Provinces, however, have no governing authority over their member dioceses.

The Episcopal Church at the Churchwide Level

Each diocese is part of the Episcopal Church in the United States of America, whose chief pastor is the Presiding Bishop. The authority of the Episcopal Church rests in the **General Convention**, the legislative body of the Episcopal Church, which meets once every three years to approve programs and budget.

Just like the U.S. Congress, General Convention is made up of two legislative bodies—the **House of Bishops** and the **House of Deputies**. The House of Bishops is made up of all bishops—both active and retired. It has about three hundred members. It meets at General Convention to consider legislation and it meets twice a year between conventions for worship, prayer, study, and dialogue. At these between-convention meetings, the House of Bishops often issues pastoral statements that offer guidance and advice to members of the church.

The Episcopal Church website, episcopalchurch.org, has a lot more information.

The House of Deputies has about nine hundred members—four clergy and four lay ministers from each diocese. Each province also sends two youth to General Convention, each of whom has a seat and voice, but no vote, in the House of Deputies. A President of the House of Deputies is elected from among the deputies. With bishops, deputies, youth, and a multitude of observers, over fifteen thousand people attend General Convention.

The Presiding Bishop

The **Presiding Bishop** is the Episcopal Church's chief pastor and representative to the world. At one time the senior bishop present at meetings was the Presiding Bishop; today the Presiding Bishop is elected by the House of Bishops and confirmed by the House of Deputies and serves for a period of nine years, or until his or her seventieth birthday. The Presiding Bishop leads the Episcopal Church by serving as its spokesperson to churches throughout the world and providing guidance and vision for the Episcopal Church. As Presiding Bishop, he or she presides at the House of Bishops and General Convention. He or she visits all dioceses of the church and is often the chief consecrator at the consecration of a bishop. As is true for all members of the Episcopal Church, the Presiding Bishop must act within the Constitution and Canons of the church.

Did You Know?

Not all the heads of churches in the Anglican Communion are elected. For example, the Archbishop of Canterbury, the head of the Church of England, is appointed by the prime minister of England.

Executive Council

Between General Conventions, the business of the Episcopal Church is carried out by the **Executive Council**. The Executive Council takes care of "the coordination, development, and implementation of the ministry and mission of the Church." That means it carries out the resolutions of the General Convention. The Presiding Bishop is the president of the Executive Council, and the President of the House of Deputies is its vice-president.

The chart on the next page is an overview of the basic structure of General Convention. The work of the General Convention is carried out by the various committees, commissions, agencies, and boards.

Budget

The annual budget for the Episcopal Church when this book went to press was about $50 million, twenty dollars for every baptized member. Episcopal parishes, on the other hand, have a total budget of

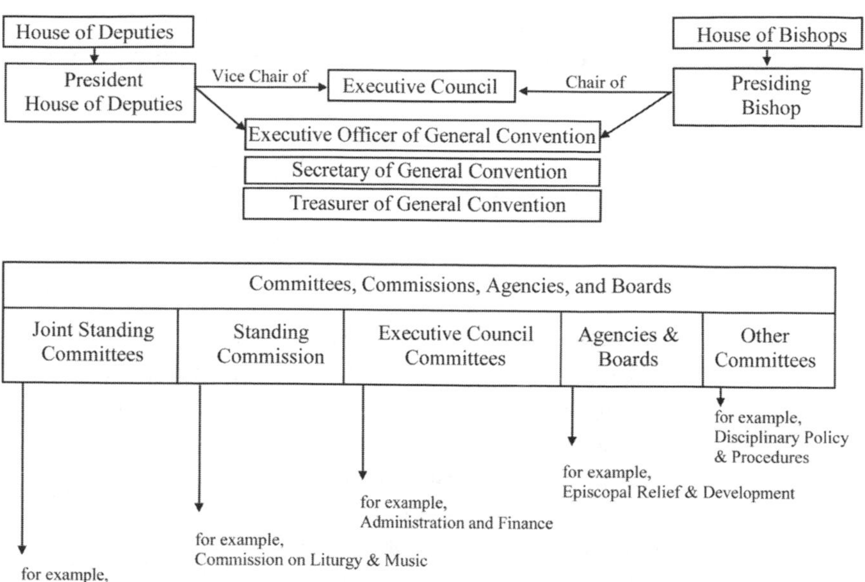

General Convention has two houses—the House of Deputies and the House of Bishops. Proposed resolutions must pass both houses to be accepted by General Convention. (The Episcopal Church Annual 2005 © Morehouse Publishing. Used by permission of Morehouse Publishing, Harrisburg, Pennsylvania.)

about $2 billion, or over nine hundred dollars per baptized member. This shows that most of the ministry of the church is at the parish and diocesan levels. Through their dioceses, parishes fund about two-thirds of the national church's budget. The rest comes from earnings from investments and government grants. The budgets reflect the priorities of General Convention, which for recent conventions have been:

- Young adults and youth
- Reconciliation and evangelism
- Congregational transformation
- Justice and peace
- Partnerships with provinces of the Anglican Communion

Constitution and Canons of the Episcopal Church

Although there is a lot of diversity within the Episcopal Church, parishes can't do just whatever they please. They live within the Constitution and Canons of the Episcopal Church. There are, for example, specific rules about marriage and remarriage as well as which prayers we can use during services. These rules aren't set in stone. Delegates can vote to change these rules through resolutions. Those passed by General Convention become **Acts of the General Convention** and govern our life as Episcopalians. Episcopalarchives.org publishes all Acts of convention.

Activity: National Canons establish the versions of the Bible authorized for use as lessons. One version is used in the Book of Common Prayer. What version is it? See "Concerning the Service of the Church" in the Book of Common Prayer.

An Example of a Resolution: The Book of Common Prayer

The Book of Common Prayer contains the liturgy, prayers, and instructions for common worship in the Episcopal Church. To be *official*, it must be accepted by General Convention. Every church in the Episcopal Church worships using the Book of Common Prayer; a priest who doesn't follow the instructions within the prayer book can be reprimanded by the bishop. But because our language and culture change continually, along with the way we understand God and the church, from time to time we change and update the prayer book. A look at the opening Prayer of the Eucharist in the prayer book of 1549 shows us the change in language:

> All Episcopal churches use the same Book of Common Prayer, which was adopted by General Convention in 1979.

> ALMIGHTIE God, unto whom all hartes bee open, and all desyres knowen, and from whom no secretes are hid: clense the thoughtes of our hartes, by the inspiracion of thy holy spirite: that we may perfectly love thee, and worthely magnifie thy holy name: through Christ our Lorde. Amen.
> (1549 Book of Common Prayer as published at justus.anglican.org)

To keep our liturgy vibrant, the Book of Common Prayer must change too. Revisions and additions to the prayer book are developed by the Standing Liturgical Commission, a group of clergy and lay persons elected by General Convention, which meets both at and between conventions. Let's consider the process that led to the 1979 Book of Common Prayer. Beginning in 1950, the Standing Liturgical Commission published a series of studies on the 1928 prayer book. In 1967, it proposed a new Rite of Holy Eucharist, which was passed at General Convention for trial use. In 1970, a series of new Rites of Holy Eucharist were passed. These new rites were used on a trial basis by a number of parishes throughout the country that gave feedback to the Standing Liturgical Commission. In 1973, additional rites and revisions, which included initiation, the Daily Office, and the Psalter, were authorized and again tried out throughout the church. In 1976, the commission submitted a draft Book of Common Prayer, which was passed as the official prayer book in 1979 under Title II, Canon 3 of the Canons of the Episcopal Church.

At each General Convention, both the House of Bishops and House of Deputies discussed the revisions and additions, and the prayer book became official when it was approved by a majority in both houses. The approval of the prayer book is a good example of the conversations among all ministers of the church, which is how the Episcopal Church is governed.

Activity: When was the first Book of Common Prayer for use in the Episcopal Church ratified? See page 8 in the Book of Common Prayer.

Anglican Communion

The Episcopal Church is a member of the **Anglican Communion**, a group of 38 independently governed churches in 164 countries that share a common faith, history, and tradition. Member churches of the Anglican Communion, such as the Church of England and the Church of the Province of Southern Africa, are called provinces. Each church has its own chief bishop, known as a **primate**, and its own rules. (The primate of the Episcopal Church is the Presiding Bishop.) No primate has jurisdiction over the members of another province within the Anglican Communion.

Anglican churches share a common history in the Church of England and express their faith, liturgy, and sacraments in a Book of Common Prayer (though not all with the same Book of Common Prayer). Four principles unite churches in the Anglican Communion:

1. the Old and New Testaments are the revealed Word of God,
2. the Nicene Creed is our statement of Christian faith,
3. two sacraments are baptism and Holy Eucharist, and
4. bishops follow a succession of ordination from the apostles to the present.
   (Chicago-Lambeth Quadrilateral, 1886, 1888, as printed in the 1979 Book of Common Prayer, 876–77).

Sharing in these principles, however, doesn't, by itself, mean a church is member of the Anglican Communion. A church is recognized as a member of the Anglican Communion when that province's bishops are invited by the **Archbishop of Canterbury** (the primate of the Church of England) to a **Lambeth Conference** and their membership is recognized by the Anglican Consultative Council. The Lambeth Conference is a gathering of all bishops within the Anglican Communion that's held every ten years at Lambeth Palace, the official residence of the Archbishop of Canterbury.

The Archbishop of Canterbury is the symbolic head of the Anglican Communion. He is known as "first among equals," which emphasizes the equality and joint authority of all primates. He can't tell any church in the Anglican Communion what to do.

The Archbishop of Canterbury, the Lambeth Conference, the Primates' Meetings, and the Anglican Consultative Council are the "instruments of unity." Go to anglicancommunion.org to learn more.

The most basic way Anglican churches express their unity is to meet for dialogue, prayer, fellowship, Bible study, and Eucharist. The Lambeth Conference is one way of doing this. Another way is the **Primates' Meetings**, an annual gathering of the primates of all provinces in the Anglican Communion. A third is the **Anglican Consultative Council**, a gathering of laypeople, bishops, priests, and deacons from churches throughout the Anglican Communion.

By gathering together as one, the Anglican Communion can work together to serve God's mission in the world. Lambeth Conference, Primates' Meeting, and Anglican Consultative Council are responsible for activities and projects such as helping to relieve suffering in the world. It also maintains the Office of the Anglican Observer to the UN to express its concerns and collect and share information about UN initiatives.

The Anglican Communion, as you can see, has a loose definition. Who belongs is determined by who attends its meetings. In the early 2000s the "bonds of affection" (sense of unity) were strained when the Episcopal Church in the United States confirmed the election of an openly gay priest as bishop of New Hampshire and the Anglican Church of Canada adopted liturgies to bless same-sex unions. In response to these events, a commission of the Anglican Communion proposed a covenant that more specifically defined what it means to be in communion. And at a Primates Meeting in 2005, the Episcopal Church and the Anglican Church of Canada were requested to withdraw their delegates from the Anglican Consultative Council until the next Lambeth meeting in 2008. The two churches withdrew from official participation, but continued to send observers. The primates continue in respectful dialogue, balancing what it means to be of one mind and the strength of unity of voice it can provide to address worldwide issues regarding human rights and poverty.

Activity: What do the Articles of Religion (found in the Historical Documents section of the Book of Common Prayer) say about the authority of the Church?

GOD'S PROMISE TO THE NEW CHURCH

After the Holy Spirit descended upon the apostles, Peter spoke to the apostles, recalling the words of the prophet Joel:

> *In the last days it will be, God declares,*
> *that I will pour out my Spirit upon all flesh*
> *and your sons and your daughters*
> *shall prophesy,*
> *and your young men shall see visions,*
> *and your old men shall*
> *dream dreams.*
>
> (Acts 2:17)

What can we learn from this sermon? After receiving the Holy Spirit, we are called to "prophesy" and "see visions." We are invited to dream God's dream of mercy and justice and prophesy to that dream. We are the active hands of Christ in the world who can work with God to bring God's kingdom near.

You are charged to do the work of the church. The structure of the church is a mechanism to do that good work. Some ways you can become involved in the structure of the church are:

- Find out if you are eligible to serve on your vestry or when you might become eligible. Consider seeking nomination. The vestry helps define how the ministry of the church is applied in your community.
- Become active in diocesan youth events such as Happening and other retreats.
- Investigate whether a youth delegation attends your Diocesan Convention and see how to become a part of it.
- Investigate the process by which your province selects its two youth delegates to General Convention and consider applying.

Dream dreams and prophesy your vision to the church. The governing bodies of the church set the policy and rules of the church so important to its ministry.

Chapter 9

What Is God Calling You To Do?

Here is my servant, whom I uphold,
my chosen, in whom my soul delights;
I have put my spirit upon him;
he will bring forth justice to the nations.
He will not cry or lift up his voice,
or make it heard in the street;
A bruised reed he will not break,
and a dimly burning wick he will not quench;
he will faithfully bring forth justice.
(Isaiah 42:1–3)

Read the passage slowly to yourself. Pause. Read it again. Then ask yourself, "Who is the servant?" What is the servant being called to do? This "Servant Song" from Isaiah was written as a call to Israel. God calls his chosen, Israel, to a mission of justice. We see this song again in the Christian Scriptures, but this time for God's servant, Jesus:

Here is my servant, whom I have chosen,
my beloved, with whom my soul is well pleased.
I will put my Spirit upon him,
and he will proclaim justice to the Gentiles.
He will not wrangle or cry aloud,
nor will anyone hear his voice in the streets.

He will not break a bruised reed or quench a smoldering wick until
he brings justice to victory.
And in this name the Gentiles will hope. (Matthew 12:18–21)

The first sentence echoes the voice of God at Jesus' baptism—"This is my Son, the Beloved, with whom I am well pleased." With delight, God claims his son as chosen and loved. The second sentence declares that the Holy Spirit has descended on Jesus, giving him the gifts to fulfill his mission—the same mission God gave to Israel to proclaim justice.

Like Jesus, God has given you a mission to bring justice to the world.

We've received that mission, too. As baptized members of the body of Christ, we inherit the role of servant. We're chosen by God and helped by the Holy Spirit to bring justice to our community and our world. Through our baptism we become Christ-bearers to the world, promising to take up Christ's mission. Israel's Servant Song is our Servant Song. Return to the Servant Song at the beginning of this chapter and read it one more time. Cross out each "he" and "him" and insert your own name. Read it again and imagine yourself as the servant of God who upholds you and whose Spirit rests on you. How does that feel? What are you called to do as a servant of God?

Parents and Mentors

Read the Servant Song together, using your own names. What could you do or what do you already do to bring justice to the world?

BAPTISMAL PROMISES

At baptism each of us made five promises, called **baptismal promises**—or someone made them for us. These are promises to do the work God has given us to do in the world—our mission. At confirmation we renew these promises by answering, "I will, with God's help":

Will you continue in the apostles' teaching and fellowship, in the breaking of the bread, and in the prayers? *I will, with God's help.*

Will you persevere in resisting evil, and whenever you fall into sin, repent, and return to the Lord? *I will, with God's help.*

Will you proclaim by word and example the Good News of God in Christ? *I will, with God's help.*

Will you seek and serve Christ in all persons, loving your neighbor as yourself? *I will, with God's help.*

> Will you strive for justice and peace among all people, and respect the dignity of every human being? *I will, with God's help.*

Our promises begin with the community—the community of Christ's body, the church—which nourishes us and supports us to keep our baptismal promises. This promise reminds us that we know ourselves first as members of a community of faith and that praying and receiving the sacraments prepares us for our work in the world. The second question reminds us that before going out in the world we must make things right with ourselves—we must live according to God's will. We promise to resist evil, and, when we sin, to turn away and return to God.

The final three promises tell us about our work in the world—how we are to be servants to others. We are to share the good news of God's love of all people both with our words and how we behave. That is, our actions are to reflect God's love. We are to seek and serve Christ in all people. Look for the goodness in others and treat others as if they are Christ himself. As Matthew's gospel says in the parable of the goats and sheep, "Truly I tell you, just as you did it to one of the least of these who are members of my family, you did it to me" (Matthew 25:40). We do this by feeding the hungry, clothing the poor, providing shelter for the homeless, and caring for the sick. In all that we do, we promise to strive for justice and peace among all people. That is, deal fairly and honestly with others and work toward bringing all people together as one community. As baptized Christians, living out these promises is our ministry.

MINISTERS: WHO WE ARE

In the last chapter you read a little about **ministry**—our ways of serving others. The Episcopal Church recognizes all baptized people as ministers in God's creation. The ministers are laypersons, bishops, priests, and deacons. Everyone who's been baptized shares a common ministry—representing Christ and his church. Laypeople also have another ministry: "to bear witness to him wherever they may be; and, according to the gifts given them, to carry on Christ's work of reconciliation in the world; and to take their place in the life, worship, and governance of the Church" (Book of Common Prayer, 855).

All baptized people are ministers in God's creation. You, too!

You are a minister. And your ministry right now is as a lay person. Ninety-nine percent of God's people are called to this important lay ministry. Read the description again and notice how it matches our baptismal promises that related to our work in the world. We're called "to bear witness to him." This is the third promise we make at baptism. We're called to "carry on Christ's work of reconciliation in the world." This fulfills our fourth and fifth promises.

Let's look at reconciliation in the world a little more closely. What does reconciliation mean? Have you ever reconciled a bank statement? You compare your written record of deposits and withdrawals with the bank's records and make adjustments to your account until the two match. Think about reconciliation in the world the same way. There are two things—the world as we actually live it and the world as God desires us to live. So the work of reconciliation is living so that those two worlds match. As ministers we're called to live in ways that make our world today match the way God wants the world to be.

God gives us gifts to fulfill our ministries. Lauren F. Winner (born in 1976) uses her gift of writing to explore issues about faith and living as a Christian in today's society. In Girl Meets God *(2003) she shares her spiritual journey from Judaism to Christianity. She was baptized in the Church of England at age twenty-one. Her writing reflects an honest desire to acknowledge and understand God's presence and call. She is also the author of* Mudhouse Sabbath *(2003) and* Real Sex: The Naked Truth about Chastity *(2005) and numerous articles.*

Activity: Which services in the Book of Common Prayer can be led by lay ministers?

ANOINTED INTO A ROYAL PRIESTHOOD

You might still feel a little uncomfortable understanding yourself as a *minister*. What makes us ministers is our baptism. Just as Jesus was anointed by the Holy Spirit when he was baptized, so were we. And after we were baptized we were anointed with oil of chrism, blessed so that everyone sealed with it shares in the royal priesthood of Jesus Christ. The writer of 1 Peter tells early Christians the very same thing: "you are a chosen race, a royal priesthood, a holy nation" (2:9).

The oil you were sealed with has a long history that symbolizes our priesthood and our ministry. Samuel poured an entire horn filled with oil on David's head to anoint him king of Israel (1 Samuel 16:13). God anointed prophets (Isaiah 61:1). A woman with an alabaster jar anointed Jesus with expensive oil before his death and resurrection (Matthew 26:7). We were anointed with the oil of kings and prophets into our ministry.

At baptism you are sealed with the oil of kings and priests.

OUR MINISTRY PROCLAIMS GOD'S DREAM FOR CREATION

So how do we live our ministry today? Many of us have loving families and friends, times when we laugh with others, basically healthy minds and bodies, and not too many roadblocks getting in the way of what we want. Others of us face difficulties—being lonely, grieving the loss of a loved one, being sick with disease, and perhaps days we don't have enough to eat or warm clothes to wear. The world falls short of what God would like. Although we may see signs of God's dream for us—like when we experience joy—it isn't here completely. To know what our ministry is, we need to understand what that dream looks like and figure out what we can do to make it happen. So, the first step is to figure out what is the dream of God.[2]

God's Dream in the Hebrew Scriptures

God is always telling us about his dreams for the world. It's a world filled with joy, a world of relationships with others, a world where our needs are met, and a world where people are honest and fair. At the beginning, God created plants and creatures of every kind, of the land, air, and sea—and then blessed them. God created humans and blessed them, too. This tells us that God wants us to be filled with life and joy. God saw that humans were lonely, and provided them with companions. This reminds us that God wants us to have relationships with other people and live in community. To each of the creatures he made—the plants, the animals, and the humans—God commanded, "be fruitful and multiply." God planned a world where there is enough for everyone. It's a world of abundance. And finally, God gave humans command over every living thing—

God longs for the world to be filled with joy, community, plenty, and justice.

2. I am indebted to John L. Kater Jr. and his unpublished work, *The Persistence of the Gospel*, for guiding much of the discussion of the kingdom of God.

not just for power, but for servanthood. God's kingdom is a world of order and service and a world of justice.

The Bible also has stories when the world was far from being joyful, abundant, and just. During these times God reminded his people about his dreams and what he longed for for them. One such time is when the nation of Israel lived in exile in Babylon and the Israelites lived in a foreign land. They lived as slaves, suffered disease, and didn't live long. But in the midst of this hardship, God sent a prophet to remind them of his love and desires. This is what God said to his people:

> Prophets are people called by God to proclaim the will of God. Examples are Moses and Jeremiah.

I will rejoice in Jerusalem
and delight in my people;
no more shall the sound of weeping be heard in it,
or the cry of distress.
No more shall there be in it
an infant that lives but a few days,
or an old person who does not live out a lifetime;
for one who dies at a hundred years
will be considered a youth,
and one who falls short of a hundred
will be considered accursed.
They shall build houses and inhabit them;
They shall plant vineyards and eat their fruit.
They shall not build and another inhabit;
They shall not plant and another eat;
For like the days of a tree shall the days of my people be,
and my chosen shall long enjoy
the work of their hands.
They shall not labor in vain,
or bear children for calamity;
for they shall be offspring blessed by the Lord—
and their descendents as well.
Before they call I will answer,
while they are yet speaking I will hear.
The wolf and the lamb shall feed together,
the lion shall eat straw like the ox;
but the serpent—its food shall be dust!

They shall not hurt or destroy
on all my holy mountain, says the Lord.
(Isaiah 65:19–25)

This song tells us more about what God's dream for the world looks like. People have no reason to weep. They live long lives, so long that those who live to be a hundred are still youthful. People live in the houses they build and eat the fruit they plant. All people are treated fairly. People do not live without because God responds to them. God's vision of creation is marked by abundance. They live in a community without enemies—where the wolf and the lamb feed together. God longs for a community of peace.

Activity: According to "A Prayer attributed to St. Francis," found in the Prayers and Thanksgiving section of the Book of Common Prayer, what can we do to be instruments of God's peace?

Jesus' Ministry Proclaiming the Kingdom of God

Jesus also tells us about what God wishes for creation. The four Gospels tells the story of Jesus proclaiming the arrival of the kingdom of God. In Mark, for example, Jesus says, "The time is fulfilled, and the kingdom of God has come near" (Mark 1:15). Jesus spoke about God's dreams as the kingdom of God, a place where God's will ruled. Jesus used the word "kingdom" because people were ruled by kings and familiar with kingdoms.

Gospel means "good news." Jesus proclaimed the good news that the kingdom of God was near.

Jesus' words and actions showed us God's dream for us by bringing joy, community, abundance, and justice to the world. One of the first things Jesus did after being baptized was to call together a community of people—his disciples. They worshipped, studied, and prayed together, and they saw Jesus performing miracles, healing, forgiving, and gathering more people together. Jesus sent this group of ordinary people to continue to do God's work in the world.

The people Jesus called were ordinary people just like us. Some were fishermen; others did work that was despised in Jewish society, like collecting taxes. They weren't the smartest or the most faithful. Lots of times they doubted Jesus, and they fought over who was the most important. They weren't very reliable, either—after all, they fell asleep in the garden the night before Jesus was crucified, even though he asked them to stay up with him. They had weaknesses just like we do. All this tells us that we too can be part of God's community. If these seemingly unworthy followers of Jesus could help bring about God's kingdom, we can too. God's kingdom is a place where we live with one another in community.

Duane Gibson, a.k.a. D.O. (born in 1978) helps bring God's dream closer by speaking with young people about his life's struggles with adversity to motivate them take on the hard work needed to achieve their goals. In his work, he uses his gifts as a rapper and public speaker. As master of ceremonies for the Hip Hop e-mass at Trinity Episcopal Church in the Bronx, NYC (HipHopEMass.org) he spreads the good news of Jesus Christ. D.O. holds the Guinness World Record for freestyle rap!

Justice

Soon after calling the first disciples, Jesus told them about the kingdom of God in the Sermon on the Mount, or the Beatitudes: "Blessed are those who mourn, blessed are the meek, blessed are those who hunger, blessed are the merciful, blessed are the pure in heart, blessed are the peacemakers, blessed are the persecuted, and the reviled" (Matthew 5). They are blessed because they will be comforted, inherit the earth, be filled, receive mercy, see God, and be called children of God. God's kingdom will be filled with justice.

Life of Joy

Throughout Jesus' ministry, he healed the sick and forgave those who had done wrong. Jesus brought them joy. What is amazing in these stories is how important touch is to his ministry of healing and forgiveness. For example, Mark tells us that he touched a leper, said, "Be made clean!" and the leper was cured. A woman who had been hemorrhaging for twelve years touched Jesus' cloak and was healed. Jesus laid his hands on the blind man to restore his sight. Touched by Jesus' healing power, these people could live out their lives with joy, free of disease. What we can learn from this is that while we might not be able to heal like Jesus, we can bring others joy by reaching out to them to let them know we care. And we can offer an embrace or handshake of forgiveness to those who have hurt us. By our touch we can bring joy to the world.

Abundance

Jesus' ministry demonstrated what life is like with abundance. When the disciples are faced with a hungry crowd of more than five thousand people and only a few fish and a couple of loaves of bread, Jesus feeds them all—with twelve baskets of food to spare. Nothing runs out. When people asked him to describe the kingdom of God, Jesus talked about abundance: a mustard seed that grows into a tree that provides a home for the birds; yeast mixed with flour that expands into nourishing bread. In Jesus' life of abundance, out of little comes much. We too can share what little we have, and together with others who have little, provide enough for everyone.

Activity: According to the parables of the mustard seed and the yeast (Luke 13:18–21), what is the kingdom of God like?

Community

Community was central to Jesus' ministry—from calling the disciples to welcoming the outcast to forgiving the sinner. Consider the story of Jesus and Zacchaeus, a tax collector, in Luke 19. As a tax collector for the Roman Empire, Zacchaeus was considered unclean and a sinner. When Jesus came to him, Jesus announced that they would dine together at Zacchaeus's house. So, even before Zacchaeus confessed his sins, Jesus forgave him and invited him into his group of friends. Zacchaeus responded by repenting and giving back what he'd stolen. By bringing these outcasts back into the community with forgiveness, Jesus gave them the strength to change their lives. Jesus' acts of forgiveness restored community and brought peace.

For Jesus, there's always more room at the table, and the community can always be expanded. In the Parable of the Good Samaritan, Jesus tells us that our neighbors are those who society says are unclean. We, like Jesus, can invite others into our community—especially those who don't seem to belong.

Activity: Read Luke 10:29–37. To whom are we called to minister? Who is your neighbor?

We, too, Are Called to Proclaim

Jesus shared this ministry with his disciples, granting them the power and authority to heal and proclaim the kingdom of God. They continued this ministry after Jesus' death and resurrection and, with the power of the Holy Spirit, baptized believers to do the same. Through our baptism we too are part of the community that has been sent out to do God's work.

We too are called to a ministry of supporting relationships within *community*. We too are called to a ministry of *abundance* by providing for the needs of others. We too are called to a ministry of *joy* by healing the sick and comforting those who are mourning. We too are called to a ministry of *justice* by treating others fairly and honestly and asking others to do the same.

It's no mistake that our baptismal promises are all about living the way God dreams for us to live. We promise to seek and serve Christ in all persons, loving our neighbor as ourselves. And we promise to strive for justice and peace among all people, and respect the dignity of every human being. We are called to do this, as Jesus did, from our community of faith. Through baptism we share in the ministry of Christ, a hands-on ministry marked by healing, forgiveness, blessing and supporting others that fulfills God's desires for creation. Through our ministry we participate in God's dream of a life of joy, community, abundance, and justice.

Our baptismal promises help us know how to live into God's dreams for us.

Kathryn Nishibayashi (born in 1982) brings joy to the world by serving the poor and homeless in Philadelphia. She spent her first year after graduating from college in hands-on ministry with Servant-Year. Participants in this intentional Christian community commit themselves to serving people in need in the City of Philadelphia. Kathryn uses her gifts of teaching and communication to help adult men who were at one time homeless master skills they need to become self-sufficient. She is bringing the touch of Christ to the world.

Where is Our Ministry?

Ministry happens wherever we are, not just in church. The mission and ministry of the people of God is out in the world. Just as Jesus sent the disciples out into the world to spread the good news, so we too are sent out to serve God throughout the week. Your ministry, then, happens at school, on the playing field, at home with your family, out with friends, and with your neighbors. Where you see people nurturing relationships and making new friendships, living a life of joy, giving generously, and acting justly, you're seeing God's kingdom being proclaimed.

Ministry happens wherever we are, not just in church.

As a community of faith, we gather each week to worship God and to study, pray, and serve together. Just as Jesus maintained a core community we too must help to nourish our central faith community. We do this in many ways. We take part in our community's worship life as acolytes, choir members, altar guild members, lectors, or chalice bearers. Or we can participate and/or lead prayer and study as a Sunday school teacher, youth leader, or member of a prayer group or a support group. We can even help at soup kitchens, tutoring programs, homeless shelters, and prisons. By continuing in worship, prayer, study, and service, we're strengthened to go out in the world in peace to love and serve God.

Activity: List one way that you act as servant to a neighbor. List one way that you act as servant to your faith community.

YOUR MINISTRY

So, what does your ministry look like? People minister in a variety of ways. Some help others as healthcare givers, some bring joy to life through music and art, some prepare people for a life of service as teachers, and still others . . . the list goes on and on. To consider how you minister, begin by remembering one way that you fulfill each of your five baptismal promises and jot it down.

I continue in the apostles' teaching and fellowship, in the breaking of the bread, and in the prayers by: ______________________________

____

One time that I persevered in resisting evil is when I: ____________

____

The last time I proclaimed by word and example the Good News of God in Christ was when I: ______________________________

____

This week I served Christ in a particular person, loving him or her as a I love myself when I: ____

____

One action I took that brought justice and peace to my community, and therefore the world, was when I: ___________________________________

____

Looking at the actions you've already taken to fulfill your baptismal promises gives you some idea of what your ministry is in the world. The way each of us answers these questions is different because each of us is uniquely and wonderfully made. Each of us has received our own unique gifts to fulfill our ministry.

You Have Been Given Special Gifts

Gifts of the Spirit are talents and abilities God gives us to fulfill our ministry.

In letters to early Christian communities in Corinth, Galatia, and Rome, the Apostle Paul wrote about **gifts of the Spirit**—talents and abilities God gives us to fulfill our ministry. Paul was addressing the struggles these communities were facing. What were their ministries? What gifts did the people have to fulfill those ministries? How could the individuals in the community work together for the same purpose? We continue to ask ourselves these very same questions. This is what we learn from Paul.

There Are a Variety of Gifts

There are a variety of gifts.
You have at least one gift.
Nobody has all the gifts.
God gives generously.
Gifts are for the common good.
Using our gifts brings joy.

There are a variety of gifts. In 1 Corinthians 12:4–10, Paul lists the following gifts: wisdom, knowledge, faith, healing, working of miracles, prophecy, discernment of spirits, tongues, and the interpretation of tongues.

And in Paul's letter to the Romans he lists these gifts: ministry, teaching, exhortation, generosity, diligence, and cheerfulness (Romans 12:6–8). Both lists addressed the needs of the communities to whom Paul had written; neither was meant to be exhaustive. The Spirit gives different gifts at different times to address the changing needs of the community.

You Have at Least One Gift

The Spirit gives a least one gift to every person. And each person's gift is different. How neat is that—to know that God looked at you and gave you your very own gift? God has entrusted you with something valuable.

Randy Greves (born in 1966) fulfills his baptismal promises as a novice in the Order of the Holy Cross. He entered the Order of the Holy Cross in 2003. He is a novice because, as of the printing of this book, he had not taken his final vows. Randy was drawn to the monastic life for a long time and spent several years exploring communities and in discernment to the vocation as a monk. His ministry at Holy Cross includes contributing to the life of the monastery in the sacristy, book shop, leading retreats, and speaking to youth and adults who work with youth in the church.

Nobody Has All the Gifts

Remember, community is important to God. So, you shouldn't be surprised to know that while everyone has at least one gift, you don't, nor does anyone, have them all. You are meant to use your gifts in community. In 1 Corinthians 12, Paul talks about a community as a human body. The body has many parts, each necessary to the health of the body but none sufficient on its own. "If the foot were to say, 'Because I am not a hand, I do not belong to the body,' that would not make it any less a part of the body"; and also, "the eye cannot say to the hand, 'I have no need of you'" (1 Corinthians 12:15, 21). Suppose the person with vision didn't share her gift. Imagine the harm a body could do if it couldn't see what it was doing. You need to use your gifts along with the gifts of others.

God Gives Generously

God provides spiritual gifts generously. You, together with others in your community, have all the gifts you need to do to make God's dream for the world happen. In fact, God gives even more than we need. Think about the Parable of the Sower in Mark's gospel (4:3–9). The farmer threw seeds all over the place—on the path, on rocky ground, among thorns, and on good soil. God is like that—giving generously and hoping that the seeds will take root. Our job is to receive God's gifts and nurture them to bear fruit. An important step in using your gifts is being confident that, indeed, you have the gift and have enough of it to be successful.

The 2004 movie *The Incredibles* shows what's possible with abundant gifts. Elastigirl, the mother and caregiver of all, needs to be able to stretch herself in all sorts of directions. And she does—she has the gift of literally stretching herself thin! Violet, the teenager who wants to blend in and protect herself from outsiders, is given her gift in such quantity that she can disappear and generate a protective force field. Dash and Mr. Incredible have oversized gifts too—overconfident Dash can run at super speeds and Mr. Incredible is super strong

Take a minute and imagine what you could do if your gifts were super-sized. Imagine that you had unlimited generosity or wisdom. What would you do differently?

What would you do differently if your spiritual gifts were supersized?

Use Your Gifts for the Good of Everyone

The Incredibles also illustrates the possibilities when we use our gifts for the good of everyone. This family works together when trouble comes. Elastigirl stretches into a parachute to save her family from falling. Violet protects herself and her brother with her gift of a force field. As Mr. Incredible says, "Having super powers is great. Having the love of family is truly powerful." We are to use our gifts not to boost ourselves, but to serve others. The Apostle Paul tells us the same thing. Each member uses his or her gifts for the good of the family, bringing the community to its greatest ability to live into their call.

Activity: Read the Parable of the Talents in Matthew 25:14–29. From this parable what do you learn about what we should do with our gifts?

You may not be a superhero fit for the big screen, but when you use your gifts in everyday acts of ministry, you're an everyday hero. What may seem like simple acts to you can be great acts of ministry to others. Think about saying a simple "hello" to someone who doesn't belong to a group at school and may feel like an outsider. That simple "hello" might just change that person's whole outlook from feeling rejected to feeling acceptable and valued.

You Bring Joy to the World When You Use Your Gifts

God created you and blessed you, and wants you, and all people, to have joy. So, using your gifts will also make you happy. Using your gifts will feel good. The Apostle Paul talked about joy in terms of the fruit of the Spirit. In his letter to the Galatians (5:22–23), he lists the following fruit: love, joy, peace, patience, kindness, generosity, faithfulness, gentleness, and self-control. All of these suggest a life of joy.

You can do an amazing number of things. In school, you have to be able to manage your time, solve math problems, read books, write essays, make robots, and analyze mold. Is everything that you *can* do a gift? No. Just because you might be good at something doesn't mean it is your gift. Gifts are something you have a passion for. Suppose you earn A's in both math and English. You can set up and answer word problems in math class. You do it well. But you do it because you have to. What you *really* like to do is to read novels and write short stories. The difference between math and English in this example is that math is a *skill*, reading and understanding the complexities of plot are *gifts*.

> Gifts are abilities that you are passionate about.

You can use your gifts for lots of purposes. You could use them to bring people together or use them selfishly for your own gain; you can use them to build relationships or to tear them down, to nourish life or to destroy it. What we learn from the Bible and the Christian community is that God gives us gifts to build community, strengthen relationships, nourish and support life, and bring people closer to God. Your gifts will help you to fulfill the promises you made at baptism and will reaffirm at confirmation. As Christians we recognize that our gifts originate with God and use them for God's purpose—the kingdom of God— not for our own purposes.

FINDING OUR SPIRITUAL GIFTS

So, each of us has gifts for ministry. And each of us has responsibility to find out what those gifts are. Once we come to know those gifts, we can nurture and honor them by offering them to God. We offer them to God by practicing them in our ministry to proclaim the kingdom of God.

Activity: Read the Catechism's answer to "What is the ministry of the laity?" on page 855 of the Book of Common Prayer. How is each of us to carry out Christ's work of reconciliation in the world?

The word "discern" comes from the Latin word meaning to distinguish. Discernment means distinguishing one thing from another thing.

The process that helps us come to know our gifts is called **discernment**. The process of discernment pulls apart the various possibilities to see each more clearly. It is a process of distinguishing the various gifts, distinguishing our gifts from those of others, and distinguishing those that are of the Spirit from those not of the Spirit.

Spiritual discernment is always done with God's will in mind. So we begin by placing ourselves before God, asking questions, and listening. You can practice the prayer exercises you learned in Chapter 7 to begin your discernment. Here are two basic questions that you can pray about as a beginning to discern your gifts.

Remember, gifts bring us joy. So ask yourself:

What do I long to do? And what are those things that bring me joy?

Our gifts are to be used for the common good—to fulfill God's dreams. So, ask yourself:

How do the things I long to do fit into God's dreams? How do they bring joy, meet the needs of others (abundance), gather community, and create a world that is fair to all people (justice)?

The work of discernment is never finished. Our gifts change, the needs of the community change, and consequently, our ministry will change. These are two very broad questions that you can continue to ask yourself from time to time.

Keilani Burroughs (born in 1988) discovered her gift for public speaking when she began reading the lessons for Sunday worship as a fifth grader in her Sioux Falls, SD, Native American congregation. She served on the Design Team for the Episcopal Youth Event (EYE) in 2005 and was the EYE the Master of Ceremonies for daily gatherings of over 1,300 EYE participants. She continues to develop her gifts by remaining actively involved in church and diocesan events.

You might want to try a more structured exercise of discernment. Here are three that will help you identify specific gifts grounded in Scripture and God's work in your life. Try each and see which one most clearly helps you find out who you are and discover what God is calling you to do.

#1 Listing Gifts

Paul listed a number of gifts of the Spirit, which provide a good beginning place. But because communities and cultures change, those gifts will also change. So, to add to and update his list, write the four characteristics of the world that God desires: life of joy, community, abundance, and justice. What abilities do you think would help someone create a world where there is less sorrow and sickness (is filled with joy), one where people relate to one another with care (has community), one where people are no longer hungry, homeless, or in need (is abundant), one that treats people fairly and honestly (has justice). Write those gifts below each quality that defines God's kingdom. Write as many as you can. Share your list with someone else. Examples are:

One exercise to discern your gifts is to list qualities that you have that bring joy, community, abundance, and justice into the world.

Life of joy	Community
Can play an instrument	Forgives
Laughs and is cheerful	Shows compassion and mercy
Comforts and/or cures the sick	Oversees projects
	Has a strong faith
	Likes to invite

Abundance	Justice
Gives generously	Knows right from wrong
Forgives	Can persuade others of what's right
Shares faith	Encourages others
Has a strong faith	Teaches truth
	Counsels others

Gifts likely fit more than one of the categories. This list that you come up with provides you with gifts that are actively used today.

#2 People We Admire

Continue with the following exercise to see which of these gifts are also likely to be your gifts.[3] Think about the people you admire and whose actions bring about a world of life in joy, community, abundance, and justice. They can be people you know personally or someone you have read about. They can be contemporary, historical—or even fictional characters from a book or a movie.

Write a list of as many of these people as you can. When you're done, underline six who especially stand out for you. Next to each name write down three or four things that you admire about this person. For example, suppose you wrote the name of a teacher who encourages you to do your best and is able to explain class material in a way you can understand. So, next to that name, you might write, *encouraging*, *wise*, and *well-spoken*. If you wrote the name of a great leader such as Mahatma Gandhi, you might write *compassionate*, *dedicated to peace*, and *perseverant* next to his name. Do this for each person you wrote down. When you've finished, look at the qualities you've named. What are the common characteristics you find among those you admire? While the people may lead or have led very different lives from one another, you will likely find similarities in their characters.

> You likely share the same gifts as those of people you admire.

What this exercise reveals are the gifts that you value and very likely have yourself. If you do this exercise in a group, you will find that no two people will have the same list. The people that you name might be similar, but the characteristics that are common to your list are unique to you.

#3 Considering Your Own Life

Already in this chapter you listed examples of how you have acted to fulfill your baptismal promises. Whether you realize it or not, you're already using your gifts. In an exercise of discernment you reflect on your actions to recognize the gifts you are already using. So, return to your answers to how you're fulfilling your promises on pages 161 and 162. Next to each write, the talent you used to fulfill that promise. If you wrote a letter to a congressperson about a homeless shelter in your town as an example of bringing justice

> Sometimes just looking at what you already do will tell you what gifts you have.

3. Based on an exercise in *Discerning Your Spiritual Gifts* by Lloyd Edwards (Boston: Cowley Publications, 1988), 55.

to the world, you might write *wisdom* and *compassion*. Be specific in your answers. How, for example, did wisdom and compassion guide you? You might say *knowledge of local housing ordinances* and *knowledge from the Bible of what Jesus asked of his community*. And you might add *sense of responsibility for the poor*. You see opportunities for ministry differently than everyone else does. Remember, no one has all the gifts—and our gifts complement one another.

You now have three lists—one that shows the possibilities, a smaller list of those gifts you see in yourself, and another list of those gifts you've already realized you have. Keep all these gifts in mind as you continue in your ministry and see how they guide you to respond to the world.

The Importance of Community

It's always important to discern our gifts within a community. We do this for many reasons. Discernment is difficult. Our community can give us guidance and perspective. Because we're human, we can be led astray by our own egos and lose sight of God's call to us. Abba Moses, a fifth-century monk living in the deserts of Egypt, told this unfortunate story of another monk, Hero. Hero believed he could discern God's call without the help of his community and so he went to live alone. After a time, Hero came to believe that God, wanting to test his faithfulness, called him to jump into a deep well. Hero jumped in the well. A few days later, the brothers found Hero and pulled him out of the well. Hero died two days later. Now, this is a dramatic story of someone hearing voices other than that of God. But we, too, can be led astray by our own desire to prove ourselves.

Our community's guidance doesn't just keep us from going astray, it also shows us gifts we might not recognize ourselves. God wants us to use our gifts in a community that has discerned God's will, and God will give us the gifts we need to do that. But we can't do it by ourselves.

Activity: What is the duty of all Christians? Look on page 856 of the Book of Common Prayer for the answer.

Ignatian Examen

Two very basic questions you can continue to ask yourself each day as a practice of discernment are:

When did I feel most alive today?
When did I most feel life draining out of me?

Ignatius Loyola, who developed the examen, was a priest who lived in the 1500s in Spain. He founded the religious order the Society of Jesus, also known as the Jesuits.

These two questions come from the practice of **Ignatian Examen**, a process an individual can use to find God's call to him or her developed by a Spanish saint named Ignatius Loyola in the early 1500s. The examen helps people understand God's desires and will for them within their daily lives. The examen is based on the belief that God actively guides us. God speaks to us both in the good and the bad times. The questions might not appear to relate to God directly. By asking God to guide us as we ask ourselves the questions and seek the answers, our reflections and answers are more likely to reflect what God wants of us. There are other sets of questions to use in the practice of examen:

For what moment today am I most grateful?
For what moment today am I least grateful?

and

When was I happiest today?
When was I saddest?[4]

The examen is meant to be practiced regularly. By asking ourselves these questions each day, we will begin to see patterns in our choices and experiences. These patterns suggest our gifts and God's call to us. As you may guess, the times when we're happiest, energized, and most grateful are likely to be times when we're using the gifts that God gave us. By asking simple questions, we can be open to God's continual call to us to be ministers, bringing our world closer to God's dream for it.

THE IMPORTANCE OF CHURCH TO MINISTRY

When you were baptized, you became a member of the body of Christ—the church. Each week we gather from our various ministries out in the world to thank God for his creation and blessings. We offer our prayers for ourselves and

The closing prayer of the Sunday service reminds us that worship prepares us for our ministry in the world.

4. These questions are from *Sleeping with Bread: Holding What Gives You Life* by Dennis Linn, Sheila Fabricant Linn, and Matthew Linn (Mahwah, NJ: Paulist Press, 1995).

others and confess our shortcomings. We ask for God's mercy and forgiveness to help us return our lives to God's way. And we're nourished by the communion bread and wine. We end our worship together each Sunday by asking for the strength to return to the world to do God's will:

Eternal God, heavenly Father,
you have graciously accepted us as living members
of your Son our Savior Jesus Christ,
and you have fed us with spiritual food
in the Sacrament of his Body and Blood.
Send us now into the world in peace,
and grant us strength and courage
to love and serve you
with gladness and singleness of heart;
through Christ our Lord. Amen.
(Book of Common Prayer, 365.)

My Faith, My Life: Glossary

Acts of the General Convention. Legislation passed by General Convention that governs the common life of all Episcopal churches.
Adoration. Words and actions that express our love for God and creation.
Advent. The first season of the church year during which we prepare for Christ's coming into the world and Christ's return.
Alb. A white garment worn by bishops, priests, deacons, and acolytes during the entire liturgy.
Altar. The table within the sanctuary around which Holy Communion is celebrated.
Anamnesis. An active form of memory that connects the past to the present in a way that allows us to become a present participant in a past event.
Anglican Communion. A group of 38 independently governed churches in 164 countries that share a common faith, history, and tradition.
Anglican Consultative Council. A gathering of laypeople, bishops, priests, and deacons from provinces in the Anglican Communion. The Anglican Consultative Council is the only incorporated body of the Anglican Communion.
Anglican prayer beads. A set of thirty-three beads joined together into a circular pattern used along with words of prayer.
Antiphon. A sentence, usually from the Bible, said before and after the psalm.
Apocalyptic. Revelatory or prophetic. Apocalyptic writings in the Bible such as the Revelation to John reveal visions of judgment and salvation.

Apocrypha. Books and writings added to the Bible in the sixteenth century by the the Roman Catholic Church. Not all Christians recognize the Apocrypha as Holy Scripture.
Apostles' Creed. The earliest formal statement of Christian belief. The Apostles' Creed is said during baptism, Morning Prayer, and Evening Prayer.
Apostolic. An adjective that describes something as continuing in the teaching and fellowship of the apostles. We say that the church is apostolic.
Apostolic succession. The passing of authority by apostles to local leaders with the laying on of hands. Episcopal bishops today are the successors in an unbroken line of ministry to the apostles.
Archbishop of Canterbury. The primate of the Church of England. The Archbishop of Canterbury is first among equals and has the right of invitation and recognition of other Anglican provinces to the Anglican Communion.
Ayres, Anne. 1816–1896. First American religious sister in the Anglican tradition. With a few other sisters organized the Sisterhood of the Holy Communion in 1852.
Baptism. Full initiation by water and the Holy Spirit into the body of Christ and the church.
Baptismal Covenant. A statement that affirms belief in the triune God followed by five promises to follow in the Christian fellowship, resist evil, proclaim the good news, serve Christ in all persons, and strive for justice and peace. The congregation renews the Baptismal Covenant with candidates for baptism.
Baptismal font. The container inside or at the entrance of a church that holds the waters of baptism.
Baptismal promises. Five promises candidates for baptism make about how they will live their lives as members of the body of Christ. See the answers to questions 4–8 of the Baptismal Covenant on pages 304 and 305 of the Book of Common Prayer.
Bible. A collection of sixty-six books of the Hebrew Scriptures (Old Testament) and the Christian Scriptures (New Testament) that reveal God's creative and redeeming actions throughout history. Also called Holy Scriptures.
Bishop. One of three ordained orders of ministry in the church. A bishop serves the offices of apostle, chief priest, and pastor of a diocese. A bishop suffragan, a bishop coadjutor, or biship assisting assist bishops diocesan in large dioceses.
Book of Common Prayer. The Book of Common Prayer provides the liturgies, prayers, and instructions so that all members of the church may share in common worship. First established in England in 1549 by the Act

of Uniformity. The American Book of Common Prayer was first adopted in 1789 by the First General Convention of the Episcopal Church.

Brent, Charles Henry. 1862–1929. A priest who led the Episcopal Church in the ecumenical movement that established the first meeting of the World Council of Churches in 1948.

Burgess, John. 1909–2003. The first African American to serve as bishop of a diocese in the Episcopal Church.

Calvin, John. 1509–1564. A French leader of the Reformation. Calvin wrote a systematic theology that rejected the authority of the pope, accepted justification by grace through faith, and expressed a fundamental doctrine of predestination. The doctrine of predestination is the belief that God directs the course of history to the minutest detail. According to this doctrine, humankind's role in creation is to maintain the order created by God.

Canon. 1. The collection of books recognized as Holy Scripture. 2. The written rules of the Episcopal Church for its governance. 3. Title of assistant priests at a cathedral.

Canticle. A "little song" based on Scripture used in worship. See pages 144–145 of the Book of Common Prayer for a list of suggested canticles for Morning and Evening Prayer.

Catechumen. Someone who is in the process of preparing for baptism. The process includes learning Christian beliefs and practices and discerning a desire to become a member of the church.

Cathedral. The designation of the church that houses the cathedra, the bishop's seat. The cathedral is the principal church for the diocese.

Catholic. A term that means universal. We say that the church is catholic because it is a faith for all people and for all time.

Centering prayer. A prayer of quieting and stillness to know the presence of God. Developed by the Desert Fathers and Mothers and revived by Trappist monk Thomas Keating.

Chalice. A cup for the wine at Eucharist.

Chancel. The area of the church that contains the pulpit, lectern, and altar, and is often raised in elevation and separated from the nave by a rail or screen. Often called the sanctuary.

Chasuble. A long poncho-like garment worn by the celebrant over the alb during the Eucharist.

Christian Scriptures. A collection of twenty-seven books written by early Christians that proclaim the good news of Jesus Christ and tell of the early history of the church.

Christmas. The season of the church year during which we celebrate the birth of Christ. It begins on Christmas Day and ends twelve days later on January 6, Epiphany.

Coeternal. Two or more things that can be understood only in relationship to one another as part of a whole. They exist together at all times into eternity.

Collect. A short prayer that "collects" the themes of the day. Collects vary according to the day, the season of the church year, and the occasion, and can be found in services in the Book of Common Prayer.

Communicant. Member of a church who has received communion at least three times in a year.

Communicant in good standing. A communicant who has been ". . . faithful in working, praying, and giving for the spread of the Kingdom of God."

Confession. Prayer in which we admit that we have done something wrong, turn away from sin, and seek to restore our relationship with others through God.

Confirmation. The rite in which a baptized person makes a mature commitment to Christ and receives continuing strength from the Holy Spirit.

Constitution and Canons of the Episcopal Church. The written rules that govern the Episcopal Church.

Corporal. A white square of cloth on which the bread and wine are placed during the Eucharistic Prayer.

Covenant. An agreement entered into freely by two or more parties. A covenant with God is a relationship initiated by God and responded to by people in faith.

Crosier. (also spelled crozier) A staff that symbolizes the pastoral ministry of the bishop.

Daily Office. A set of prayers and readings that mark the times of the day.

Daniels, Jonathan. 1939–1965. A young European-American Episcopal Seminarian martyred in the Civil Rights movement.

Deacon. One of three ordained orders of ministry in the church. A deacon is called to be a servant to those in need and to assist the bishop and priests in proclaiming the gospel and administering the sacraments.

Dean. The lead clergyperson at a cathedral.

Diocesan Convention. Annual meeting of representatives from all parishes within a diocese. Similar to an annual meeting for a parish, but for the diocese.

Diocesan Council. A group of priests and lay persons elected from within a diocese along with the bishop to act on behalf of Diocesan Convention during the year.

Diocese. Basic administrative unit of the Episcopal Church. Individual churches act in accordance with the rules of, and share a common mission with, their diocese. The jurisdiction of a bishop diocesan.

Discernment. A process of understanding. As a Christian practice, discernment is a process of prayerful reflection in which we come to understand our spiritual gifts and God's call to ministry.
Easter. A season of the church year during which we celebrate the resurrection of Christ. Begins with Easter Sunday and lasts fifty days.
Enmegahbowh. 1807–1902. First Native American priest ordained in the Episcopal Church. Worked among the Ojibway peoples in Minnesota.
Epiclesis. Words that ask God to send the Holy Spirit to make the bread and the wine holy so that they will be the body and blood of Christ.
Epiphany. The day on which we celebrate the visit of the Magi to the Christ Child. Also a season of the church year in which we celebrate the divinity of Jesus beginning with Jesus' baptism and ending with the Transfiguration.
Epistles. A set of twenty-one writings, many which are in the form of letters addressed to early Christian communities or individuals. The Epistles are part of the Christian Scriptures.
Executive Council. An elected body of people charged with "the coordination, development, and implementation of the ministry and mission of the Church." It acts on behalf of General Convention.
Fasting. Actively choosing not to do something for a short period of time so that we may draw our attention to God.
Fraction anthem. A hymn sung at the breaking of the bread.
General Convention. The highest legislative body of the Episcopal Church, which meets once every three years to approve the Episcopal Church's programs and budget.
Gifts of the Spirit. Talents and abilities God gives us to fulfill our ministry.
Gloria. A song of praise to God in the service of Holy Eucharist.
Gospels. Four books in the Christian Scriptures (Matthew, Mark, Luke, and John) that proclaim the good news of salvation through Jesus Christ by telling about Jesus' ministry, teaching, death, and resurrection.
Great Commandments. You shall love the Lord your God with all your heart, and with all your soul, and with all your mind and you shall love your neighbor as yourself.
Great Commission. The charge by Jesus in the Gospel according to Matthew to the disciples to "go and make disciples of all nations."
Great Thanksgiving. The name given for the Eucharistic Prayer. Also known as the prayer of consecration.
Harris, Barbara Clementine. 1930–. First woman consecrated bishop in the Episcopal Church. Consecrated bishop suffragan of the Diocese of Massachusetts in 1989. Known also for her commitment to civil rights issues and justice.

Hebrew Scriptures. A collection of thirty-nine books that form the first part of the Bible and tell the stories of the Hebrew people and their covenant relationship with God. Also called the Old Testament.

Henry VIII. 1491–1547. King of England who issued the Act of Supremacy, which made the king the head of the Church of England and severed the ties between the Church of England and the Roman Catholic Church.

Hobart, John Henry. 1775–1830. Led early efforts to grow the Episcopal Church. During his time as bishop of New York, the number of churches in his diocese more than tripled and the number of clergy quintupled.

Holy Eucharist. The principal act of Christian worship in which we remember the life, death, and resurrection of Jesus Christ and proclaim that we await his coming in glory.

Holy Matrimony. The physical and spiritual binding together of two people before God and his people for mutual joy and with the intention of a lifelong commitment.

Holy Spirit. God's power and presence in our history, in our present, and in our future. The Holy Spirit is the third person of the Trinity.

House of Bishops. The gathering of all bishops at General Convention to consider legislation and between conventions for worship, prayer, study, and dialogue. The House of Bishops also meets twice each year between General Convention and often issues pastoral statements that provide guidance and advice to the church.

House of Deputies. One of two legislative bodies of the Episcopal Church. (The House of Bishops is the second legislative body.) The House of Deputies is comprised of a group of clergy and laypeople elected by the Diocesan Convention in every diocese.

Icons. Visual images that point beyond themselves. Icons are commonly used in the practice of prayer.

Ignatian Examen. A specific process of discernment developed by Ignatius of Loyola in the sixteenth century based on the belief that we can understand God's desires for us in the context of our daily lives.

Incarnation. The belief that Jesus was God in the flesh.

Intercession. Prayers in which we request God's blessings and grace for others.

Invitatory. A sentence and response that opens our hearts and minds to the purpose of the gathering.

Jesus Prayer. A mantra, "Lord, Jesus Christ, son of God, have mercy on me, a sinner."

Jones, Absolom. 1746–1818. First African American priest ordained in the Episcopal Church. Born a slave, he bought his own freedom and the freedom of his wife. With Richard Allen, Jones established the Free African Society, the first organized African American society in the United States.

Justification by grace through faith. A doctrine set forth by Martin Luther that salvation is a gift from God. Individuals need only respond in faith to accept salvation.

Kairos. A quality of time in which past, present, and future are experienced in one moment.

Kemper, Jackson. 1789–1870. Kemper became the first missionary bishop in 1835, and served in the western territories of the United States during the mid-1800s. He encouraged the translation of services into native languages and pleaded for more attention to Native Americans. His unofficial title is "The Bishop of the Whole Northwest."

Labyrinth. A sacred pattern in the shape of a circle with one path that winds to the center and back out again. A famous labyrinth is the eleven-circuit labyrinth on the floor of Chartres Cathedral in France.

Lambeth Conference. A gathering of Anglican bishops held every ten years at Lambeth Palace, the official residence of the Archbishop of Canterbury.

Laypersons. The people of God called to carry on Christ's work of reconciliation in the world according to the gifts given to them. Most of the ministry of the laity occurs outside the church. Lay persons may also perform ministries within the church.

***Lectio divina*.** A four-step process of prayerfully reading the Word of God. Lectio divina is a method of reading for prayerful devotion rather than scholarly study.

Lectionary. A three-year cycle of Scripture readings for use in public worship. The Book of Common Prayer includes two lectionaries—a lectionary for Sundays and the Daily Office lectionary. Many Episcopal churches follow the Revised Common Lectionary for Sunday readings.

Lent. The season of the church year during which we prepare for the resurrection of Jesus. It is a time of prayer, fasting, and penitence. It begins on Ash Wednesday and ends on Holy Saturday, the day before Easter.

Liturgy. The rites (prayers) and actions that define our common worship as a community.

Luther, Martin. 1483–1546. A German leader of the Reformation. He posted ninety-five theses on the door of the castle church in Wittenberg, inviting others to oppose practices by the Roman Catholic Church. One particularly abusive practice he opposed was the church's selling indulgences to sinners as proof of their repentance necessary for salvation. One of Luther's more famous doctrines is the doctrine of justification by grace through faith. This doctrine stated that sacraments, good works, and the

mediation of the church were not necessary for salvation, and put individuals in direct connection with God.
Mandala. A circular pattern of lines and colors used as a tool for prayer.
Mantras. Sacred words or phrases said repeatedly for a period of time.
Memorial. An act or object that preserves the memory of a person or event. In the context of Eucharist, memorial is declaring that Christ is among us, a living sacrifice, for us today.
Memorial Acclamation. Words of praise by the people (Christ has died. Christ is risen. Christ will come again) said after the words of institution during the Great Thanksgiving.
Middle Ages. A period of time from the fall of the Roman Empire in the fifth century to the rise of the Renaissance in the fifteenth century. During the Middle Ages there was a strict division of social classes and land was largely controlled by nobles and the church. Without a strong and stable political force, Christianity became the leading force in Western civilization.
Ministry. The Christian calling to serve.
Miter. A tall, pointed hat worn by the bishop. (Also spelled mitre.)
Monastic community. A group of people who believe in God and live in community with others separate from society and who dedicate themselves to simple lives of service and prayer ordered by a common rule of life.
Muhlenberg, William Augustus. 1796–1877. Leading priest in the Episcopal Church in the nineteenth century who was concerned that the church minister to all social groups.
Nave. The large vertical area of a cross-shaped church where worshippers gather. The nave lies between the chancel and the narthex.
New Covenant. The relationship established with God through Jesus Christ in which God promises to bring us into the kingdom of God. We promise to believe in Christ and keep his commandments to love God and our neighbors as ourselves.
New Testament. See Christian Scriptures.
Oakerhater, David Pendleton. 1850–1931. First Cheyenne deacon in the Episcopal Church. He founded schools and missions throughout Oklahoma.
Old Covenant. The relationship God established with the Hebrews in which he would be their God and they would be his people. They promised to love justice, do mercy, and walk humbly with their God.
Old Testament. See Hebrew Scriptures.
Opening acclamation. The greeting to God's family that begins the service of Holy Eucharist and proclaims in whose name we gather.

Ordination. The sacrament by which God gives authority and the grace of the Holy Spirit through prayer and the laying on of hands to those being made bishops, priests, and deacons.

Oxford Movement. A movement in the nineteenth century to revive earlier Roman Catholic liturgical practices.

Parables. Stories used as metaphors for teaching. The Synoptic Gospels present Jesus as teaching with parables.

Parish. A group of people who have incorporated as a congregation within the church who worship regularly, participate in the sacraments, and support one another in their Christian lives.

Paschal Triduum. The three days of Easter. Begins with the Maundy Thursday service in the evening, peaks with The Great Easter Vigil, and ends with the celebration of the Eucharist on Easter morning.

Paten. A small plate for the bread at Eucharist.

Pentateuch. The first five books of the Bible: Genesis, Exodus, Leviticus, Numbers, and Deuteronomy. The word is derived from two Greek words—*pen* meaning "five" and *tecuho* meaning "book."

Pentecost. The fiftieth day after Easter on which we celebrate the birth of the church. Also, the season after Pentecost and before Advent.

Petition. Prayer in which we request God's blessings and grace for ourselves.

Prayer. The experience of the presence of God through words, actions, or silence. Forms of prayer are adoration, confession, thanksgiving, intercession, and petition.

Presiding Bishop. The national church's chief pastor and representative to the world.

Priest. One of three ordained orders of ministry in the church. Priests administer the sacraments, proclaim the gospel, serve as pastor to the people, and, with the bishop, oversee the church.

Primate. The chief bishop of a national Anglican Church. The primate of the Episcopal Church is also called the Presiding Bishop.

Primates' Meetings. An annual gathering of the primates of all provinces in the Anglican Communion.

Psalms. A book of hymns in the Bible. Psalms is the only book of the Bible included in its entirety in the Book of Common Prayer.

Rainsford, William. 1850–1933. Episcopal priest active in social ministry in the late nineteenth and early twentieth centuries.

Real Presence. The belief that Christ's body and blood are present in the consecrated bread and wine. By eating the communion bread and drinking the wine we are made one with Christ.

Reconciliation of a Penitent (also just reconciliation). The sacrament of confessing one's sins to a priest and receiving assurance of pardon and the grace of absolution.
Rector. A priest who leads a parish church.
Reformation. A religious movement of the sixteenth century that began as an attempt to reform the Roman Catholic Church and resulted in the establishment of Protestant churches. The Reformation addressed what were perceived to be abuses of power by the Roman Catholic Church that had developed during the Middle Ages.
Ritual memory. The recollection of actions that deepen our experiences as they are repeated.
Robinson, V. Gene. 1947–. First openly gay priest to be consecrated a bishop in the Episcopal Church. Consecrated the ninth bishop of the Diocese of New Hampshire in 2004.
Rubrics. Directions for liturgies printed in italics in the Book of Common Prayer.
Rule of life. A set of guidelines for living that aid in keeping our lives in balance with God as the center.
Sacrament. An outward and visible sign of inward and spiritual grace, given by Christ as sure and certain means by which we receive that grace. (See the Book of Common Prayer, page 857.)
Sanctus. A hymn of praise beginning with the words "Holy, Holy, Holy" and sung during the Great Thanksgiving.
Seabury, Samuel. 1729–1796. The first American bishop of the Anglican Church. Consecrated by Scottish bishops in November 1784.
Season after Pentecost. The weeks during the church year after Pentecost Sunday and before the first Sunday of Advent. The Season after Pentecost is a time for growing in faith.
Shema. The Hebrew declaration of faith in one God: Hear, O Israel: The LORD is our God, the LORD alone (Deuteronomy 6:4).
Sin. Falling short of God's will.
Spiritual direction. The art of helping others explore a deeper relationship with God.
Spiritual disciplines. Intentional practices that keep us in dialogue with God.
Stole. A narrow width of cloth worn by bishops and priests over both shoulders and by a deacon over the left shoulder.
Sursum corda. A Eucharistic dialogue between the celebrant and the people in which the people lift their hearts to the Lord. The *Sursum corda* begins the Great Thanksgiving.

Thanksgiving. Prayer in which we express our gratitude to God for all the blessings and mercies God gives us.
Transept. The horizontal parts of a cross-shaped church extending out from the nave and the chancel.
Transubstantiation. The belief that when consecrated, the substance of the bread and the wine are transformed into the substance of Christ's body and blood, while the appearance as bread and wine continues to be unchanged.
Trinity. The belief in one God who exists in three eternal, distinct, and equal persons.
Trisagion. The prayer, "Holy God, Holy and Mighty, Holy Immortal One, Have mercy on me."
Tyndale, William. 1494–1536. First person to translate the Bible from the original Hebrew and Greek into English.
Unction of the Sick. The sacrament of anointing with oil in which God's healing grace is given to heal the spirit, mind, and body. Also called healing of the sick.
Vestments. Special clothing worn by leaders of worship. The celebrant, for example, wears a chasuble during Holy Eucharist.
Vestry. Leaders of a parish elected to supervise and make decisions, particularly about the finances and buildings and grounds, between annual meetings. The vestry also provides the planning and organization needed to support the mission of a local parish.
Words of institution. The words that tell the story of the Last Supper.
World Council of Churches. A fellowship of more than 340 churches worldwide that works toward the unity of the church.
Worship. A response of praise and thanksgiving to the God who creates us, blesses us, and loves us.

References

The Anglican Communion. Pamphlet. Communications Department of the Anglican Communion, 2004.

Artress, Lauren. *Walking a Sacred Path*. New York: Riverhead Books, 1995.

Bass, Dorothy C., and Don C. Richter. *Way to Live: Christian Practices for Teens*. Nashville: Upper Room Books, 2002.

Bauman, Lynn. C. *The Anglican Rosary*. Telephone, TX: Praxis, 2003.

Berlin, Adele, and Marc Avi Brettler, eds. *The Jewish Study Bible*. Oxford: Oxford University Press, 2004.

The Book of Common Prayer. New York: Church Publishing, 1979.

The Budget for the Episcopal Church, 2004–2006. General Convention.

Cavaletti, Sofia. *Living Liturgy: Elementary Reflections*. Chicago, IL: Liturgy Training Publications, 1998.

Constitutions and Canons Together with the Rules of Order for the Government of the Protestant Episcopal Church in the United States of America Otherwise Known as The Episcopal Church. New York: Church Publishing, 2003.

Coogan, Michael D. *The New Oxford Annotated Bible, New Revised Standard Version with Apocrypha*. Oxford: Oxford University Press, 2001.

Edwards, Lloyd. *Discerning Your Spiritual Gifts*. Cambridge, MA: Cowley Publications, 1988.

The Episcopal Church Annual. Harrisburg, PA: Morehouse Publishing, 2005.

Episcopal Fast Facts. Pamphlet. Office of Communications of the Episcopal Church, 2003.

Farrington, Debra K. *Hearing with the Heart: A Gentle Guide to Discerning God's Will for Your Life*. San Francisco: Jossey-Bass, 2003.

Farrington, Debra. "Balancing Life by the Rule." *Spirituality & Health*, Winter 2001, page 44.

Ferlo, Roger. *Opening the Bible*. Boston: Cowley Publications, 1997.

Foster, Richard J. *Celebration of Discipline*. New York: HarperCollins, 1988.

Gomes, Peter J. *The Good Book: Reading the Bible with Mind and Heart*. San Francisco: HarperSanFrancisco, 1996.

Grenz, Linda. *Doubleday Pocket Bible Guide*. New York: Galilee Trade, 1997.

Guenther, Margaret. *The Practice of Prayer*. Vol. 4 of The New Church Teaching Series. Cambridge, MA: Cowley Publications, 1998.

Hatchett, Marion J. *Commentary on the American Prayer Book*. San Francisco: HarperCollins Publisher, 1995.

Jones, Tony. *Soul Shaper*. Grand Rapids, MI: Zondervan Publishing House, 2003.

Kater, John L. *The Persistence of the Gospel*. Unpublished manuscript.

Keating, Thomas. *Open Mind, Open Heart*. New York: Continuum, 2000.

Klein, Patricia S. *Worship without Words*. Brewster, MA: Paraclete Press, 2000.

Kujawa-Holbrook, Sheryl, ed. *Freedom Is a Dream: A Documentary History of Women in the Episcopal Church*. New York: Church Publishing, 2002.

Lee, Jeffrey. *Opening the Prayer Book*. Boston: Cowley Publications, 1999.

Lesser Feasts and Fasts 2005. New York: Church Publishing, 2005.

Linn, Dennis, Sheila Fabricant Linn, and Matthew Linn. *Sleeping with Bread: Holding What Gives You Life*. Mahwah, NJ: Paulist Press, 1995.

Mays, James L., ed. *Bible Commentary*. San Francisco: HarperSanFrancisco, 2000.

Platter, Ormonde. *Many Servants*. Boston: Cowley Publications, 2004.

Post, W. Ellwood. *Saints, Signs, and Symbols*. Harrisburg, PA: Morehouse Publishing, 1962, 1974.

Smith, Margin L. *Reconciliation: Preparing for Confession in the Episcopal Church*. Boston: Cowley Publications, 1985.

Stravinskas, Peter, M.J. *Understanding the Sacraments: A Guide for Prayer and Study*. San Francisco: Ignatius Press, 1997.

Thompsett, Fredrica Harris. *Living with History*. Boston: Cowley Publications, 1999.

Webber, Christopher L. *Welcome to the Episcopal Church*. Harrisburg, PA: Morehouse Publishing, 1999.

Winner, Lauren F. *Girl Meets God: A Memoir*. New York: Random House, 2002.

Index